THE BATTLEFIELD GUIDE TO LIFE

THE BATTLEFIELD GUIDE TO LIFE

WAR STORIES AND LIFE LESSONS FROM JULIUS CAESAR TO SERGEANT YORK

JAMES K. TURNER

ACADEMY PARK PRESS
Franklin TN

ISBN: 978-1732227507 (Paperback)
ISBN: 978-0997069044 (Hardcover)

Printed by Academy Park Press, in the United States of America.

First printing edition 2018.

Academy Park Press
1314 Columbia Ave.
Franklin TN, 37064

Dedication

To Ella, my best girl

To Cal, that's what matters

Contents

Introduction

I'm just an ordinary guy, and, as an ordinary guy, I can tell you that there are two things guys never need: directions and advice. That is, until we're lost. Take that literally and figuratively because that's when we're ready to talk. The reality is that when guys open up, we typically like to walk ourselves around a subject. We tend to talk about the problems that "a friend" is having, and we usually prefer analogies to our problems. Cars are always great for that. What guy hasn't compared his girlfriend to a Porsche or a Honda. Sports are the same, and I can't count how many times I've heard friends relate some aspect of their life as the time for a Hail Mary pass, or the bottom of the ninth inning with the bases loaded. It's not that guys are superficial, and it's not that we're afraid to discuss our emotions and problems. We just feel more comfortable talking about life in such a way, and there's absolutely nothing wrong with that.

But I'm a historian, and I've always felt more comfortable using analogies from history, usually from the military aspect. In fact, the life lessons that most of us need to understand are often the simplest. They align perfectly with actual lessons that can be learned from the battlefields and the soldiers.

A look back at military history provides tremendous examples of success and failure that might serve to guide us in the future, if only as counterparts to events that we are experiencing in our present lives. For centuries people have succeeded—and failed—because of the basest of human emotions and actions. In the lives of men, some of the most important decisions, at least on a personal level, have been made on the battlefield. When your very life is at stake, you will call on all your knowledge, experience, and strength to emerge victorious. If not on the side of victory, you at least seek to survive—to fight another day, as the saying goes. The side of success involves attributes such as patience, anticipation, education, innovation, cognizance, audacity, leadership, and fortitude. The side of failure showcases arrogance, impulsiveness, inexperience, incomprehension, cowardice, indecisiveness, and misplaced trust.

The philosopher C.S. Lewis said that courage is not simply one virtue, but the form of every virtue at its testing point. That's true. There's a touch of courage and a quality of heroism in our daily conquering of obstacles in our path, as noble as those of the man who faces war and death. But can our daily struggles ever mirror those of the soldiers on the battlefields of history, who took a chance with every movement, every decision, they made? Absolutely yes, because courage is as important in your personal life as it is on the battlefield. It takes a certain amount of courage to get through life. You strive, you try, you fail, and you learn. Eventually you improve, you achieve, and you soldier on.

"The battlefield is a scene of constant chaos. The winner will be the one who controls that chaos, both his own and the enemy's." So said Napoleon Bonaparte, the epitome of a military leader who, at times, exhibited almost all the attributes of success and failure. His words still carry weight. Life is a battlefield, and it's up to us to recognize the chaos of what's happening in our world. Most of us are constantly dealing with bosses and budgets, love and romance, health and weight, friends and family, and with that intangible search for what it is that makes us who we are and what makes us happy. In the end, our success is directly linked to how we react to the chaos that comes our way and how we prepare for whatever life throws at us. Like Napoleon and all great military leaders we can, and should, use our ability to study the past and take our life lessons from those who went before. As they say, life's too short to make all the best mistakes yourself.

The summer before I started high school, I was given the opportunity to participate in a student exchange program and was fortunate enough to stay with a great family in Mexico City. They were perfect hosts, and over the first few weeks they took me to practically every tourist destination in the city. One day, after we had exhausted all the normal tourist sites, they asked if there was anything in particular that I'd like to see. I asked if there were any battlefields nearby. I was told the story of Montezuma and Cortez and taken to a museum to see magnificent remnants and artifacts from the days of the Aztec Empire. Yet what I most remember, even after all this time, is our trip to the huge Chapultepec Park where I stood on the spot where the Mexican army attempted to hold back United States troops during the Mexican-American War in 1847. Near the end of the battle six young Mexican cadets leapt from the castle walls to their deaths, rather than surrender. I stood there, captivated as I heard their story, trying to imagine the thoughts of young boys who would do such a thing. One had even wrapped himself in the flag as he jumped rather than see their colors captured. Today they are remembered as Los Niños Heroes (the Boy Heroes), and they are memorialized with a monument inside the park. We spent the rest of the day in the amusement park, but even while riding the most amazing roller coaster I'd ever seen, my thoughts were still falling back to the battle. How could boys, practically my age, sacrifice it all like that?

On that day my fascination with war went beyond the battlefield strategies and tactics that I loved to read about. My interest suddenly rose to the level of trying to understand the thoughts of the combatants and their leaders. That became what really intrigued me. I've been captivated by the psychology of war since that day, decades ago, in Mexico City. I've traveled to a tremendous number of battlefields and I've learned from each one. I don't like the idea of brave men dying, but to stand on a battlefield and observe the hills that protected them or the river that thwarted their escape is truly the best way to learn from their experience. It's possible to capture a glimpse into the past and feel a slight touch of their world as they gave their full measure.

My grandmother, a teacher, was always glad to indulge my interests. I remember a trip with her to Kentucky to see the battlefields at Perryville and Fishing Creek, where her grandfather had fought. A few years later we spent two weeks on a trip through Tennessee, Mississippi, Louisiana, and Alabama, and that was possibly the greatest trip of my life. "Mima" told me family stories, taught me old songs, and was as interested in the history as I was. We visited old houses, seemingly stopped at every roadside marker, and never passed up fresh peaches or peanuts.

But more than anything, we walked the battlefields: Shiloh, Parker's Crossroads, Vicksburg, New Orleans, Corinth, and on and on. After each of our stops, she would ask me what I learned. We didn't talk much about which unit was stationed at what point, or who their general was, to be honest. Rather, we talked about the fears the men must have had in that specific battle or the tactics that helped them anticipate what their adversary might do. Had I been in their place, what would I have done? Again, she asked, "What did you learn about them, and how will understanding their experience help you?"

In 1992 I joined a reenacting unit called Huwald's Battery, and for years we gave an incredibly accurate depiction of a Confederate mountain howitzer unit. Our battery had a couple of cannons and was mule-driven, making it a favorite with the crowds. We participated in everything from small living histories up to large reenactments with thousands of "soldiers" and tens of thousands of spectators. I loved them all. While being on the field was the most exciting part of the day, we all enjoyed the camaraderie of the evenings as we relaxed around the campfires. There, we'd often start discussing the battle we were portraying, and usually progress to others from all across history. I remember one night when we were all throwing out lessons that could be learned from various battles, and the conversations were just like those that I had been having with my grandmother. I remember thinking, "One of these guys should write a book about that!"

A few years later the topic arose again. I was talking with Gene, an old friend and one of my fellow gunners from Huwald's Battery, about a project we'd been working on. We felt that we were getting distracted by irrelevant details when we simply needed to be moving forward. We began to use the Battle of

Shiloh as an analogy for what we were dealing with. In that 1862 battle, the Confederates got bogged down for hours fighting at the Hornet's Nest when they could have just bypassed that section of Union troops. That delay, and their reluctance in pressing the battle on the first day, gave the Union the opportunity to secure Pittsburgh Landing and bring in about 20,000 additional troops overnight. That turned the tide in one of the early battles of the American Civil War, and the suddenly outnumbered Confederates were defeated and forced to retreat. We decided that we should avoid our own version of the Hornet's Nest and address our obvious priorities. Then, as we wrapped up that conversation, I said that I always thought it would be interesting to read a book based on the personal lessons that we might learn from military history. Gene agreed and then suggested that I write it. I loved the idea, if nothing more than the chance to complete the conversations I'd had with my grandmother and my reenacting buddies.

You're about to read some intriguing war stories—all true—and I've paralleled them to life lessons that I hold substantial in my own world. I hope you enjoy these vignettes from the past. My real intention is that they'll simply reinforce the positive aspects of the successful life you're already leading. These stories should not be interpreted as a glorification of war, but they can be taken as a preparation for the battlefield of life. The reality is that as long as there are people, with all our base emotions, there will be war. It is left to us to contemplate and capture the lessons from both the victors and the vanquished, and the best we can do is to learn how to survive on the figurative battlegrounds on which we tread every day. Life is a battlefield, and you can be more than a survivor. You can be the victor.

I

YOU CAN BE EXTRAORDINARY: THE MEUSE-ARGONNE OFFENSIVE

"What lies behind us and what lies before us are tiny matters
compared to what lies within us."
Ralph Waldo Emerson

In 1911, my grandmother was born into a large, poor family. The American Civil War had ended less than 50 years earlier, and its effect was still being felt in her small hometown. Her town was like most of rural Tennessee with its economy primarily based on agriculture. Farmers were still using mules, horses, and simple farm implements to raise small crops of tobacco and corn. She did have the opportunity for some basic schooling, and her oldest brother taught her how to read. She remembered the day, as a child, when that brother came home from a party and told their father that he was joining the Marine Corps. The potential adventure of the Great War had captured his imagination. She recalled that her father paced across the front porch all that day, madly chewing and spitting tobacco while she just watched.

My grandmother did eventually receive a more formal education. After completing grammar school, she attended the two-year high school program in her hometown. Because she felt that she hadn't learned enough, she voluntarily repeated those two years. Incredibly, she then completed two more years of high school, away from home at Baxter Seminary. There, she earned her room and board by getting up early in the morning and making biscuits for the breakfasts of the other students. Her dream was to become a teacher, and teaching did become her profession for several decades. She taught in Granville, where she had been raised, and her goal was to give students the finest possible education. In the early days of her career, she was often the one who brought water into the classroom or wood for the wintertime stove. Those chores were just part of the job, and she was glad to do them.

When I went to school we had a much nicer building, but there were still only two teachers for all eight grades. One classroom was for grades one through four, and it was called the Little Room; the other classroom was for grades five through eight, and it was called the Big Room. My grandmother taught the Big Room students, and she was also the school principal. When students completed eighth grade at our little school, they rode in a big yellow bus to a high school that was a 30-minute ride away, up and down steep Tennessee hills complemented by curvy roads. I know that everyone in my community was proud of the education that we received from the teachers at Granville Elementary School. Many people would look at the place and see just a small country school with, at most, maybe 60 children. There was no gymnasium; our basketball court was dirt, and the goalposts were not even equal in height. The property sloped, so when we played baseball, the outfielders were always looking up to see the batters. Home runs were not uncommon, but baseball gloves were.

I look back on those days, and can now more easily see the incredible lengths to which our teachers went for us. I can only imagine what privations they endured in the decades before I was taught. Our teachers were dedicated, smart, and relentless in pursuing their goal—that their students would learn and make better lives for their families. My grandmother, even when she was nearing retirement, continued to take correspondence courses. She was always looking to increase her knowledge and improve her methods. She set an example, a high standard for students and teachers alike, but would never have thought of herself as anyone special. Like her, you will have chances in your life to make a difference. Sometimes an average person will find himself able to change the world in a way that he never thought he would. However, when he steps forward and makes that difference, he becomes a hero of sorts. To me, my grandmother and the other teachers at Granville Elementary School will always be heroes. They were extraordinary.

*****

James K. Turner

The Meuse-Argonne Offensive — 1918

"There are no extraordinary men...just extraordinary circumstances
that ordinary men are forced to deal with."
Admiral William F. Halsey, Jr.

Some people think that heroes are born, while others say they're made. I believe that heroes are neither born nor made, but that they're all around us, merely waiting. I've read several interviews with wartime heroes, and they usually speak as if they never really had a choice with their actions. In American history there are two heroes that quickly come to my mind. The first is a Texas boy named Audie Murphy who made a gallant standalone defense against German soldiers in WWII. He became so famous that he made himself into a movie star, even once portraying himself. The second is a Tennessee backwoodsman who didn't want to go to war, but decided that it was his duty, and then made a name for himself as a Doughboy in WWI. He wasn't interested in fame or the movies, but allowed himself to be portrayed on the silver screen as a way to help raise money for education in his rural area of Tennessee.

***

Their orders were to circle around the hillside and do something—anything—to silence the heavy machine guns that had their compatriots pinned down. As impossible as the task had sounded, the American troops had somehow passed through the enemy lines and, amazingly, had chanced upon the headquarters of an enemy battalion while its men were having breakfast. To top off their improbable luck, this small detachment had discovered a unit that somehow seemed to think that it was so far in the rear as to not need its weapons nearby. It was a surreal scene, and as the Americans rushed in with guns drawn, the Germans could do nothing more than put their hands in the air while shouting "comrade!"

Just as the Doughboys were securing the enemy battalion, their quarry dropped to the ground, and one of the heavy machine guns on a nearby hill opened fire on the Yanks. That sudden burst of machine gun fire was devastating. The platoon's strength was suddenly cut in half and its sergeant terribly wounded. The men hit the ground and took cover among their prisoners. Their corporal was now in charge, but, in the confusion, he had become separated from the rest of the troops and now found himself alone on the hillside. Most soldiers would not have had a chance in the open, especially armed with only an Enfield rifle and a Colt automatic pistol, but 30-year-old Corporal Alvin C. York knew that God was on his side. He also knew that he was one of the best marksmen in France. But while this place looked so much like his native hills of Tennessee, today would not be one of those fun little shooting matches he typically won back in Pall Mall. Still, his men needed him, and he faced forward, waiting for his chance.

It was October 1918, and the Great War had been raging for four years. For the allies, primarily French and British on this front, trench warfare had become almost a way of life. Ground was taken, then given. Hills designated only by numbers were sought after for the placement of heavy guns, while men were sent "over the top" with rifles and bayonets and some insane speculation that enemy machine guns were not as effective as they had been the day before. Casualties had risen to a number beyond belief. For the Germans the same was true, but for them there was also the recognition that they were soon to bleed out. Bulgaria was suing for peace, and Austria-Hungary had practically disappeared as a military force. Their last line of defense had been the Siegfried Line, but, with any luck, they could hold their ground.

But now to the battlefield marched the American Expeditionary Force, a million-man army intent on reaching Berlin in weeks, if not days. While the French and British had been fighting the war for years, the United States had maintained an isolationist stance, and its entry into the war was very belated. Most of those gung-ho, green troops were soon to discover that their enthusiasm and excitement could be easily tempered. The Americans were commanded by General John "Black Jack" Pershing, and it was his intention to lead them as a cohesive unit, and not simply as filler troops for the depleted ranks of the Allies. The Americans had contributed successfully at Cantigny, and the Second and Third Divisions, along with their intrepid Marines, had made their name at Belleau Wood. The Allies ordered Pershing to take over the Meuse-Argonne sector, but first allowed him to lead his First Army against the Saint-Mihiel salient, which had long been a German stronghold. In conjunction with four French divisions, the Americans took just two days to push back an enemy that had been embedded there for what, to the French, had seemed like an eternity.

The next job would not be so quick or simple. The Meuse-Argonne, in northeastern France, was a vital location for the Germans because of its proximity to the railroad, which provided access to their front lines. The Germans were determined that they would hold that line. Named after the nearby Meuse River and the Argonne Forest, this part of the country was unaccustomed to battle. It still held a fair amount of cover within its hills, and there remained a sufficient number of trees and a significant screen of brush. Though the situation of the German front line was precarious, the soldiers there were experienced and well-equipped. Pershing held the view that all a soldier needed was a rifle, a pistol, and the bravado to give the Huns the bayonet—that should be enough to prevail in battle. His European counterparts knew better. The Americans were about to meet their toughest fighting yet.

The Great War had brought many changes in tactics and technology, and the ever-expanding cemeteries stood as proof to the success of those changes. When the war began, it was almost as if the soldiers were fighting in an earlier time. The French had insisted on their traditional red trousers, and, in the early days of the war, some units would have looked almost as if they were stepping forward at Waterloo a century earlier. Scotsmen, as brave as William Wallace ever was, crossed "No Man's Land" in kilts, with bagpipes playing. Germans wore their leather pickelhaubes, those traditional spiked helmets, while men from all across Europe went to war in whatever might have been handy. But those affectations could not last. In short order, all sides were adopting metal helmets, drab colors, and battlefield tactics that employed everything from deadly gas to airplanes, from field telephones to creeping artillery barrages.

Into this ever-evolving battlefield came the Americans, with their Montana Peak felt campaign hats, fashionable tunics, canvas leggings, and poor understanding of the tactics required in this new style of war. The Western Front soon mandated certain concessions, and those eponymous campaign hats gave way to a simple helmet. Canvas leggings transformed into spiral wool puttees, and the officers' tailored clothing was abandoned for enlisted uniforms. Almost all Americans now carried the same pack, haversack, and gas mask.

The American mobilization had been quick, especially considering the number of men to be raised, equipped, and trained. The logistics of carrying them across the Atlantic Ocean, which was patrolled by German submarines, were daunting. Just the same, at the height of deployment more than 10,000 American troops were landing in France every day. The Americans needed equipment, everything from helmets to heavy machine guns, and the practical solution was to buy what they needed from their allies. Therefore, the doughboys often found themselves moving to the front with unfamiliar arms, such as the French Chauchat and Hotchkiss, or the British Vickers and Lewis machine guns. Only later in the war were they primarily issued the more familiar Enfield and Browning.

The Meuse-Argonne battlefield was a funnel of sorts, and the American army was heading north, right into the teeth of the German army. The surge ahead would lead the Doughboys into three distinct enemy lines—named after witches in Wagner operas—and their untried commanders and inadequate tactics would be sorely tested. The "Whizz-Bangs" of the enemy artillery could kill a soldier before he even knew that a shell was coming at him. The water-cooled Maxims and their hundreds-of-rounds per minute of enfilading fire were just as deadly and even more maddening. Pistols, rifles, heavy machine guns, howitzers, field artillery—was there any way through the barrage? In fact, one of the best ways to break the lines of machine gun fire was to send a small unit around the base of a hill, then flank it while the machine gun nest was being held down with unceasing howitzer fire.

On this day, the 328th Regiment of the 82nd Division—known as the All-American Division—was sent forward to capture an enemy-held hill as part of an effort to rid the Argonne woods of its German occupiers. There was supposed to have been an artillery bombardment by the Americans, but it never happened. Undaunted, the 328th went forward, regardless of the circumstance that it would be walking directly into the fire of the enemy's heavy machine guns. The Americans soon found themselves pinned down on three sides, so a small unit was sent around the flank with the hope that it could take out some of the opposition. The platoon of 17 men was led by Sergeant Early, along with Corporals York and Savage, and they advanced forward through the fog and sleet of a miserable, cool morning. Amazingly, they were able to work themselves behind enemy lines. Rather than approach directly across the ridge line, they decided to advance even further and take the enemy from the rear. Quickly moving forward, the Yanks stumbled into a German camp, and it was hard to determine which group was the most surprised. The Germans were a relief unit that had exhausted itself marching up the previous night, and the men had insisted on laying aside their weapons to have breakfast before they went to the front. Seeing the Americans burst through so quickly, Lieutenant Paul Vollmer, commanding the 1st Battalion of the 120th Württemberg Landwehr regiment, felt they were being hit by a large enemy wave and surrendered himself and his men. Sergeant Early and his troops had the advantage for the moment, but recognized the danger—that they were in an almost impossible position. It's great to capture prisoners, but to do so behind the lines is almost certainly an exercise in futility. That's just what their action was then. A prisoner shouted something in German, and the Americans watched the Germans hit the ground, as machine gun fire from a nearby hill raked their position. Sergeant Early was severely wounded, his men were scattered or holding close to prisoners, and Corporal York had somehow been separated from his men.

Corporal York realized that he had suddenly become the leader of the platoon and, more importantly, recognized their dire straits. They were behind enemy lines, they were outnumbered and outgunned, and they had lost their commander. But York would do what he had to. He recognized that the enemy seemed to be confined to a hillside and, despite their numbers and guns, he had to fight. He would give it his all, his last measure, if need be.

Alvin York was a product of the backwoods of Tennessee, and, even among the sharpshooters back in those hills, he was one of the best. York had learned every aspect of the firearms that had been given to him in France, and he knew his new guns as well as any old Kentucky Rifle back home. The Germans on the hillside had the American platoon pinned down, and though the men from both sides were intermingled, they intended to make quick work of the job. It wouldn't be that simple. When the Germans hit the Americans with their initial fire, the results were devastating. Corporals Savage and York were best friends, and when the sudden burst of machine gun fire hit, dozens of deadly rounds hit Savage, practically stripping him of his clothing. The surviving members of the platoon ducked down with their prisoners, including the German Lieutenant Vollmer. Purely the result of good luck, Alvin York was positioned on a slope a slight distance away, able to view the German hillside entrenchments. As the

Germans rose above their earthworks to take shots, they did so independently, one by one. And as each man raised his head to take a shot, Corporal York was ready. Because of his fortunate location on the hill and his uncanny accuracy he could, in his own words, "touch them off."

Simply, the German soldiers had to raise their heads into line of sight if they wanted to fire down at York and the Americans, and York's rifle was ready every time. He did not want to kill those men, but he had no choice, and he did not miss. For minutes, and through several rifle clips, York kept shooting. As he shot, he continually yelled for them to surrender—to "come on down." But they were hardened men and they would not give up. Because he realized that this style of fighting was devastating them, the German lieutenant in command of the machine gun nest ordered a bayonet charge. He and five of his men went over the wall and sped down the hill, intending to close with the rifleman. When he saw this incredible act of bravery, York pulled his pistol and fired six quick shots, taking down all six attackers. He later explained that when he saw the men coming at him his actions were almost a reflex. York began his shooting by aiming at the man in the rear of the group, then moving forward to the officer in front. His tactic was based on one of his old turkey hunting tricks, ensuring that they wouldn't get spooked by seeing the man in front of them fall. Had they stopped running they would surely have crouched, taken aim, and killed him. But the charging Germans may have never found the chance to shoot, and York certainly did not miss.

The previously-captured Lieutenant Vollmer had seen all he could stand, and he worked himself toward York, telling him that he could make the machine gunners surrender if only he would stop firing. York was absolutely agreeable to this proposal. With a signal from Lieutenant Vollmer, the Germans abandoned their weapons and came down from the machine gun nest. One man who could not stomach the thought of surrender tossed a grenade at York, but it was ineffective, and York "touched him off."

It was now obvious to the Americans that the trek back to their own lines would be like a hike through Hell. The German commander suggested that they go back through the trenches, but York, relying on his common sense, would have none of that. On the way back to the American lines they constantly encountered German soldiers, but with York second in the line, his pistol pressed against the back of Lieutenant Vollmer, surrender became the norm. When they safely arrived back at the American lines, York and his men were credited with having captured 132 prisoners, making this one of the most incredible actions of the entire Meuse-Argonne offensive.

Corporal York was extraordinary that day, even beyond his marksmanship and coolness under fire. In his early years, Alvin York had been a hard-drinking hellion, but he underwent a religious conversion in his late twenties. From that transformation arose a conviction that violence and war were wrong, to the point that he wrote on his draft card that he didn't want to fight. York made a slight attempt to stay home, which was refused, and he eventually concluded that he had a duty to serve. Alvin York was extraordinary in that he was even on the battlefield, and as a member of a team that was willing to do whatever it took for success.

It's entirely possible that most of us are "wired" to be extraordinary. How many times have you read the news article about a man running in and saving the people in a burning house, with no regard for his personal safety? Then, in an interview after the fact, he says he was just doing what any normal person would do. While that's not necessarily true, in his mind it is, because he's extraordinary and doesn't realize it.

York felt that he was only doing his job, and the reality is that he was right. Any man in his unit would likely have done the same, given the opportunity and the ability. Before he ever got to that battle, however, York had spent countless hours working with his weapons and making them as familiar to himself as possible. In battle, he consistently reloaded his rifle as each clip emptied, and his ability to transition from rifle to pistol, and back again, was an action that represented his education, training, and practice. Further, he used his cognizance to safely guide his men back to their lines.

Soon promoted, the world came to know him as Sergeant York, recipient of the U.S. Medal of Honor and the French Legion of Honor and Croix de Guerre. He was famously portrayed on the silver screen by Gary Cooper, one of the biggest stars of that time. Yet he always saw himself as a country boy who did what he had to, and he used his fame and resources primarily to create schools in his rural Tennessee community. Opportunities to make a real difference arise daily, and you need only the ability to recognize when it's your chance. Be prepared, and you can be extraordinary.

2

HAVE A COURSE OF ACTION: THE BATTLE OF CULLODEN

"Setting a goal is not the main thing. It is deciding how you will go about achieving it and staying with that plan."
Tom Landry

There's an old axiom that says those who fail to plan are actually planning to fail. Like most catchy, old sayings this one usually holds true. A plan is a guidebook to your future and a road map to your dreams. Likewise, a dream without a plan is just a wish. From the simple list you take with you while you're running Saturday errands, to the game plan for your daughter's soccer game, to a corporation's business plan and mission statement, plans are critical. The successful person will put their plans and objectives into writing and will execute that ambition to the best of their ability, with the understanding that—well, simply put—circumstances change. That undeniable fact may be frustrating, but it's important to take the time and effort, regardless. The lack of a plan usually shows someone who's lazy, uncertain, or just a little too self-assured to their abilities. Even when properly developed, a plan is only as good as its execution, and fear sometimes gives us a tendency to wait and wait. General George Patton said that a good plan, viciously executed now, is better than a perfect plan next week. He was entirely correct.

Emily is a friend whom I've known for about a decade, and her success is a testament to the power of planning. She started work as a receptionist and shipping clerk, with a little bit of "everything else" thrown in for good measure. While she did those jobs, she learned everything she could about all the other aspects of the company. Obviously smart, genuinely nice and well-spoken, it wasn't long before management realized that she had skills and intangibles they needed. She learned and developed a plan to step into something better for herself. When opportunity arose—a rare opening in sales—she was able to immediately transition into that role. She was ready to handle almost any problem that was thrown at her, and, in fact, she became the "go-to guy" for half the sales team when things got complicated. She's one of those rare people that just doesn't get rattled very often, and, when she does, she will not let you see it.

But, even as she was becoming a linchpin in her employer's company, she was actively developing a plan to become her own boss through a side business as a cosmetics consultant. She chose cosmetics because it was something to which she already had a predilection, and the company she chose allowed her to establish and grow her business while she held on to her "real" job. She planned makeup parties, developed an amazing network of team members, and established a great presence on social media. Her husband is a great guy, fully supportive, and her efforts were paying dividends. In fact, as she had hoped, she soon found herself at the point where she could legitimately explore the idea of stepping out on her own. Her husband would continue to work, and with that as a safety net of sorts, she was ready. There were no guarantees, but because she had earlier outlined her strategy and goals, she soon accomplished what she had hoped to as a consultant. She was also able to recognize where she stood on the time line to her objective.

Then came the twist, because that's just the way life seems to work for us when things start to go well. Her husband's employer offered him a buyout if he would take an early retirement, giving him an opportunity to further his education and transition into a career more to his liking. Ordinarily, the choice would have been a "no-brainer," but the timing was terrible for them, because it meant that Emily likely would have to put her dreams on hold. If he were to be a full-time student, even with the buyout, someone had to be bringing home a steady check.

They sat down and talked about it. Putting pen to paper, they worked on budgets, strategies, plans, and objectives. When they were done they saw the buyout as an opportunity to move forward, and they embraced the concept that their goals hadn't changed, though their plans must. It wouldn't be easy, but they had their road map to success.

Robert Burns, the great Scottish poet and lyricist, wrote a sublime work entitled *To a Mouse*. While out plowing his fields, he accidentally destroyed the nest of a mouse which it needed to survive the winter. As he stood in the field and watched the mouse scurry away, he composed the work in his native Scots. It included one of the most famous lines of poetry ever written: "The best-laid schemes o' mice an' men, gang aft agley." Or, as we typically hear it in English: "The best-laid plans of mice and men, go often askew."

Count on the fact that life will go "sideways" for you sometimes, but when that happens, simply keep in mind your ultimate objectives and alter your plan as need be to get you there. The interesting part of Emily's story is that I must label it "to be continued," but with the firmest conviction that I know how the story will end. As I write this she's still working her "real" job, but her consulting work has brought her a new car and her husband is closer than ever to his second career. Today he's suffering through creative writing and she's still effectively working two jobs, but their goals will be met. They have the plan, the strategy, and the objective all laid out. That's what it takes to be in control of your life, and you owe it to yourself to do the same.

*****

The Battle of Culloden — 1746

"In preparing for battle, I have always found that plans are useless,
but planning is indispensable."
Dwight D. Eisenhower

If you have a goal that matters to you, then it's worth the time and effort to put together a well-developed plan. Draw a road map from where you are now to where you want to be. The map, in this case, is a written plan setting out the markers that you'll need to pass to get to your goal. Be careful, too, about delay. There are more paths to your goal than you might imagine at the start. If one option fails, you must be able to anticipate that failure and move on. One of the most important aspects of that road map to your goal is that it also allows you to plot out alternate routes. It takes effort, but it also saves you from heading down the wrong path at the very beginning. Even the best plan doesn't guarantee success, but lack of a plan likely guarantees failure.

I'm hard-pressed to name a successful military campaign that didn't begin with a well-thought-out course of action. I can, though, name more than a few when an army fought and won against equal or superior odds simply because its commanders had planned. But, show me a leader who has done little planning, can't seem to explore alternatives, or ask for advice...and I'll show you one of the most interesting stories from British history.

***

The sound of cannon fire from his own line was a surprise, but the reply from across the field was not. Lord George Murray reined his horse to the left, spun in his saddle, and attempted to gain a better understanding of where the enemy cannon shot had landed. The shot apparently had gone to the rear—his prince would be in danger—but that was a worry he couldn't entertain at this moment. His Atholl men were the right flank, anchoring on a wall and preparing for an assault, and his primary concern was that his front lines were not parallel with those of the enemy. This was not as he had planned, and he recognized that a staggered assault under these conditions, while already facing greater numbers, would potentially be suicidal. Still, the men serving under Lord George had proved their bravery time and again on other battlefields; they were merely waiting for the word to advance. On the far left of the line the MacDonalds were balking, and for their hesitance they were receiving blistering musket fire. The Highlanders to their right and toward the center were screaming with rage as they, too, were facing cannon and small arms. They were no longer able to wait for word from the prince to move forward or the signal (Claymore!) to reach their ears. Lord George spurred his horse, shouted the advance, and his Scotsmen went forward across the moor toward the British soldiers aligned against them. Armed with firelock pistols, knives, and swords, clad only in their kilts and defended solely by their round shields, they ran forward as a fury of Highland plaid that would not stop until they smashed into the Redcoats. The English receiving the charge did not understand the Scottish Gaelic, but the sentiment was clear. The stories were true and madness itself was about to lay upon them. To the rear, Charles Edward Stuart—Bonnie Prince Charlie—was led away to a safer place. Still in his mid-twenties, his appearance was that of a genteel sort, but he possessed an audacity that would not be restrained. He could perceive the wave at the front of his beleaguered army, and, as one of his guard was decapitated by an English cannonball, he could hear the screams from the front. This was not as he had hoped, not as he had planned. Rain and sleet complemented the atmosphere of the harshness that would come this day. This desolate moor in northern Scotland was witnessing the last great charge of the Scottish Highlanders.

It was April 1746, and another Jacobite Rising was in full force.

Called "The '45" for the year it began, Prince Charles Edward Stuart had prevailed through a succession of advancements and battles. Only a few months earlier he and a handful of men had arrived on the shores of western Scotland with the hope, and little else, of crowning his father as king of Scotland and England. His grandfather had once been king, but was exiled from England due to his Catholicism. His father, James, had attempted to lead his own rising in 1715, but that was short-lived and unsuccessful. Prince Charles, known as The Young Pretender, had faith in his ability to do what so many had told him could not be done. But, again and again he had demonstrated himself to be more than capable.

When the prince and his entourage landed on that barren coast of western Scotland they did so clandestinely, without even his father knowing of their plans. In fact, he didn't really have a plan and was operating almost entirely on hope and intuition. Scotland had always been favorable to the Stuarts, and the prince landed with the thought that they would be as much so in 1745 as they had been in the past. As he raised the Jacobite standard, a red flag with a white square in the center, he fully expected the support of all Highlanders and trusted that more men would rally to his cause as his presence became known. He also hoped, as his newly recruited army grew, that France would keep their implied promise to assist with money and men.

As with so much of European history this period was one in which France and Britain schemed against and warred with each other. This time the fighting was a residual of the War of Austrian Succession. British soldiers were on the continent and it seemed a perfect opportunity for the French to support anyone who might invade Britain, thereby requiring the British to recall home their men. Further, it was to the advantage of the French to establish an English king who would be their ally, if not their subordinate. The Jacobites, the supporters of James as king, were potentially strong enough to have an impact on the British population. With French assistance and an uprising among the general population, there potentially could be enough support for a king to replace George II.

But there were also skeptics. Many Scots viewed the prince as rash, speculating as to why he had practically come alone. They wondered where the French were in this latest scheme and were hesitant to be part of a losing cause as they had been 30 years earlier in "The '15." The British government forces were stronger than ever, and, to contain and quell the thoughts of future uprisings, forts had been built and manned throughout all of Scotland. Some Scots were bound to support the government, and families and clans would likely be split. Many were also concerned that this would be a fight pitting the Stuart Catholicism against the country's Protestants. In effect, this effort had all the makings of a civil, as well as a religious, war. The prince had barely considered these objections and was surprised that some Highland clans, as well as lowland Scots, stood against him. Even those who supported his cause, though, begged him to retire until another time—the odds against success were just too great. He convinced himself, even though he had established no actual course of action, that once his army took Scotland and moved south that even the English would rally to his standard.

For their part, the English first viewed the prince's arrival with disdain; his was a losing and laughable proposition. London newspapers made jokes and printed cartoons making light of the prince, as well as the Highlanders who had begun to follow him.

The Highlanders dressed differently in their plaids and they spoke another language, their native Gaelic. Perhaps they were fierce, but they could not even begin to fight properly trained and accomplished British soldiers. For his part, the English king, George II, didn't even bother to bring back troops from the continent. Lieutenant General Sir John Cope commanded the British army in Scotland and he would handle this matter quickly and efficiently. He held no real concern.

Against all odds, and almost purely through persuasion, Bonnie Prince Charlie had gained not just a following, but a fighting force. Many Highlanders held a sympathy and a dedication to King James and they would follow his son. They came from the hills and the heather. They were an army. They marched to Edinburgh, the capital of Scotland, and had the gates opened to them as the crowds cheered. The castle itself never relented, but never mind; there were balls and portraits and a widespread welcoming of guests and supporters at Holyrood Palace. More importantly to the business at hand, French King Louis XV sent money, arms, and military advisers.

Learning of this, British General Cope halted his proposed advance to the north of Scotland and set himself to what he thought would be a perfect battleground, just to the east of Edinburgh. But the Highlanders used a bit of stealth to advance on the government troops, and then with a traditional Scottish charge they smashed into and defeated Cope's soldiers. In less than fifteen minutes they had gained an incredible victory at Prestonpans, horrifying the English. The unexpected—the unthinkable—had happened.

Prince Charles called for a council of war, thinking this would be the perfect opportunity to invade England. The Highland

Chiefs were against leaving Scotland at that time, preferring to wait, strengthen their position, and then develop a specific plan of action. But they were outvoted, and their army of 5,000 trudged south toward London. England was wide open and the advance south suddenly seemed logical, as they met with successes at Carlisle, Preston, and Derby. It appeared to Prince Charles that London was so close, and he convinced himself that a continued march into London was the next logical step. But while he was, himself, convinced, not all others were. The reports were that Cumberland and Wade's armies were both searching for them and that an unknown third army was north of London. The odds were just too great and the numbers and circumstances were against the Jacobites. Lord George Murray argued that, even if the incredible odds favored them and they took London, they would be in effect walking into a cage. Another council of war was held, and, against the prince's wishes and his vehement arguments, they decided to return to Scotland. And with good reason.

The purported army north of London did not actually exist, but the other two most certainly did. King George II had finally seen the danger and called for the return of his son, complete with his large army, from the continent. Prince William Augustus, the Duke of Cumberland, had military experience, and many saw him as the savior of England. Prince William was practically the same age as his cousin (and nemesis) Bonnie Prince Charlie, but he was more rotund, with brash features and without the dash or deportment of Charles. Yet what he did have was the discipline to stop and develop a plan. Arriving back in England, he gathered his army and cavalry about him and waited for ample supplies and rations. A march into Scotland was never easy, and with the winter of 1745 approaching, he wanted to have everything in order. In fact, he even schooled his men as to the best way to rebuff a Highland charge, such as the one that had devastated General Cope at the Battle of Prestonpans. The Highland charge typically consisted of men firing their rifles and pistols, then rushing into the enemy lines with dirk and broadsword at the ready. Many Highlanders carried round shields called targes, and would use them to push enemy rifle barrels into the sky, while dispatching the soldiers with their blades. Cumberland, ever the tactician and administrator, instructed his men to stand firm, then as the charge came to them, to bayonet the enemy that was fighting the soldier to their right. That would require a large amount of trust, but would give them the ability to place a bayonet into the side of the man who would be raising his arm to strike their comrade. Though the technique was surely questioned among his men, the concept was valid and served as a reassurance that they could stand against such a maniacal charge.

The Highlander army needed more men. These men would likely have to come from Scotland, as the French seemed to be unable, or unwilling, to provide more troops. Jacobite leaders, such as Lord George Murray and Lord Elcho, argued to their prince that, even if they were able to defeat Cumberland's army, their own losses would likely be so large as to render themselves a Pyrrhic victory—a victory in name, but with terrible losses among their men. While Bonnie Prince Charlie seemed to prefer the advice of his French adviser, the persuasiveness of Lord George won out this time, and the march home continued successfully. Returning to Scotland, they gained another victory at Falkirk, and with that accomplished, decided to continue north toward Inverness—a wise choice at that time of year.

Winter in Scotland can be brutal, and for the Jacobite soldiers of 1745-46 it was even more so. Many soldiers had deserted the cause. A large number were starving, several had family who needed them, some saw this effort becoming a losing cause, and others had little trust in their leaders. To their credit, though, a large number did see it through as best they could, as they looked forward to spring. Their advance north continued and they took Inverness, charging into the town as the government forces were retreating over the bridge at the River Ness. The successes at Scottish towns like Falkirk and Inverness buoyed their hopes, and, with better weather soon to arrive, perhaps their optimism and opportunity would both increase.

As he got closer to Inverness, Bonnie Prince Charlie sent his officers to search for a field on which to fight. The French adviser chose Drumossie Moor above Culloden House, but, when Lord George Murray, a Scotsman, saw the field, he professed that there could be no worse place for a Highlander to battle. The ground was flat and firm, which would instead be an advantage to British cavalry and cannon. He strongly advocated for somewhere with hills that would be conducive to the Highland method of fighting, and boggy, to limit the magnificent British cavalry.

It seemed obvious that the Jacobites would have the worst of it in a normal fight, so they mounted a surprise nighttime advance against the government forces who were camping in the distance, celebrating Duke William's 25th birthday. But the British camp was a long walk through difficult terrain, and the Scots stumbled and slowed through the darkness. By the time the first Jacobite had almost reached the British camp, it was too late. Their line was just too extended, they were fatigued, and the day would soon be breaking. Lord Murray sent them back toward camp while the prince, who had been toward the rear of the line, protested at what he saw as an unnecessary retreat.

With the night attack unsuccessful, they returned to the moor and prepared to fight. Morning found men scattered everywhere, though, looking for food, as the logistics of supply had left them starving. Many of the men who had spent the night marching toward the British camp were purely exhausted. Some gathered themselves to the security of stone walls for sleep, while others literally fell into ditches as they walked.

Still, the bulk of the Highland army did not flee, and they stood firm on the moor, waiting. Their lines were facing north, yet the left flank of their front line was at least a hundred yards back from where it should have been. The left flank consisted of men from Clan MacDonald, furious that they were not on the right of the line where they had traditionally been since the time of Robert the Bruce. The front of the line consisted of the heads of the clans, proudly displaying their elaborate shields and broadswords, which were soon to meet the enemy. They stood with their henchmen and listened to their pipers play tunes such as "The King Shall Enjoy His Own Again" and "Hey Johnnie Cope." Blue flags with white and yellow saltires fluttered in the sleet of the cold April day, and the varying patterns of tartan reflected the variety of material available across Scotland.

The British soldiers, resplendent in their eponymous scarlet uniforms, with their own drummers and pipers playing, wheeled into place in a magnificent maneuver usually seen only on parade grounds. Their predominate flag was the Union Jack, complemented by a variety of banners across the field. Noticeable among the government troops were hundreds of Scotsmen, loyal to the established crown, and differentiating themselves from their kilted cousins sometimes only by a black cockade placed on their bonnet. The Scots on the Jacobite side sported a similar cockade, but white, on their person. The Scotsmen in the government ranks consisted of a considerable percentage of Highlanders, mostly Presbyterians. Some were there to settle old grievances, others to fight Catholics. As might be expected, though, there were also families pitted against each other. Brothers faced each other across that field, and Lord Kilmarnock, who had gone for the prince, knew that his son was on the British side.

To the center of the Highland army was a small contingent of cavalry and about 500 Irish Piquets who had been sent by the French. The prince was in the back with his bodyguard, which was a poor location for him as he was the commander of the entire army for this battle. A Highland cannon fired the first shot, which was promptly returned by the government, and the fight was on. The signal to advance was to have come from the prince, but there were delays and mistakes, and the kilted warriors stood and suffered as cannonball and grapeshot ripped through their bodies. They could take no more.

The men in the center ran forward and slammed into the British line, followed closely by Lord George Murray and his brigade on the right. The fighting was brutal and deadly here, yet men were somehow able to break through the first British line. On the left, the MacDonalds were refusing to go forward, still stung by the slight of having been placed to the left. Their commander begged them, even promising to change his name if they would advance, but there they stood. He finally went forward, practically alone, and was killed. This did have the effect of energizing the men to fight, but it was too late, and they could not close with the

British. Bonnie Prince Charlie rode to the center of the battlefield to rally his men, but there was no pathway to victory on this field. English cavalry began circling toward the Jacobite rear and enfilading fire from Major James Wolfe's troops began to devastate the Highland right flank. Lord George Murray lost his horse and his wig, but not his life, and somehow escaped the melee at the front.

It quickly became obvious that the battle was lost for the Highlanders, and the distraught prince had to be taken from the battlefield against his will. This result was not as he had envisioned, and he was unsure what to do next. Lord George felt that he had the men to continue the fight at a different time and place, but watched his army dissolve as the prince fled, having given no practical instruction to his commanders.

The audacity of Bonnie Prince Charlie had been replaced with fear as well as a feeling of frustration and loss, and his only desire was a safe return to France. As the victorious British troops laid waste to the countryside and its inhabitants, the best the prince could do was run and hide and hope that he would not be betrayed before he could slip away to the continent. He had fought his last battle; the Rising had ended, and the Stuarts were never again to return to the throne.

The Battle of Culloden is filled with irony, and the largest bit may be that Culloden was the only battle that Prince Charles ever lost, while it was the only one his cousin Prince William ever won. But Prince William had planned extremely well for this battle, and it was possibly the finest course of action ever set for a campaign on British soil. To contrast, Bonnie Prince Charlie took a bad situation, failed to listen to experience when selecting the battlefield, and then relied on the basest of plans. And I'm being lenient in calling what he did a plan.

It may be somewhat presumptuous to suggest that a Jacobite plan would have made a difference in this battle, but I do know that the Highland way of fighting, with their bravery and audacity, did have a modicum of success in a different setting. The lack of a plan is inexcusable, and while you may convince yourself that you can "play it by ear," you'll soon realize that the winners of the world will have a business plan, a budget, a method to their madness, or whatever best suits their ultimate goal. Stop the laziness, put your plan to paper, and get to work.

3

TURN WEAKNESSES INTO STRENGTHS: THE BATTLE OF COWPENS

"My attitude is that if you push me towards something that you
think is a weakness, then I will turn that perceived weakness into a
strength."
Michael Jordan

I have a great group of friends: nurses, teachers, accountants, musicians, machinists, engineers, doctors, farmers, lawyers, and jacks-of-all-trades. One of the most interesting and amazing parts of my world is the opportunity to just sit and talk with my friends, and to learn from those who do things I never could. It's not that we always talk work, but regardless of the topic, they bring forth a perspective on life that I might not otherwise have. While they are a diverse group, in general, there is one thing that I find in common among them: over time, they've all gravitated toward what they do best. I was recently having dinner with a buddy from high school, a physician, and he told me that of all the things he's learned, the most important is that he must be open to asking for professional help. His greatest moment of understanding was that it's a strength to know when to ask for a second opinion, and for assistance when he isn't comfortable in a situation. He's right, and he was exceptional in admitting that. Too often we don't want to acknowledge our weaknesses.

Yet we all have strengths and weaknesses, and most of us recognize that fact. To be sure, we've all seen the terrible karaoke singer who closes his eyes and imagines himself as the next Justin Timberlake. Or the want-to-be successor to Julia Roberts struggling to remember her lines at the local community playhouse. But those folks are quite rare. Typically, even children gravitate toward the soccer team, the cheerleading squad, the band, or the sidelines—they know what they like and where they excel. It's not an innate recognition, necessarily. Most of us discover our strengths through experience. You may really want to be a star pitcher, but by ten-years-old you'll know whether you'll ever throw a blistering fastball right over the plate. If you're not supposed to be on the mound, then explore the idea of becoming a catcher, utilizing your knowledge of pitching to help out the guy who can "bring the heat."

Several years ago, I was sent out to work a trade show in California, an event large enough that our company wanted to also bring in a local sales representative. John was one of our best outside salesmen—one of the two best in the country—and

I was excited about getting the chance to see how he did it. We'd talked often by phone, and had even met a couple times, but I'd never had the opportunity to see him interact with customers. The software program we were selling was extremely user-friendly, but also comprehensive enough to meet the design needs of architects, builders, and related trades. As the show started, I was looking forward to watching this whiz-kid dazzle potential customers with the nuances and in-depth possibilities our program could offer.

Instead, I watched as he demonstrated the program in much the same way as I did. To be honest, within a couple hours I began to realize that he wasn't much better with the program than I was. It seemed as if he spent as much time shooting the breeze with folks as he did demonstrating the program. I had seen some of our other sales reps in the field, people with incredible technical knowledge of the program, and that's what I was expecting here. I fully thought I would witness the reincarnation of Frank Lloyd Wright...but, no. I just could not understand how this guy was out here selling it. Heck, not just selling, but SELLING!

I had to ask. I don't recall my exact words, but they were probably something like, "Not to be insulting in any way, but you're one of our best sales guys, and I'm not sure that you're much better at this program than I am." And his reply was, "I'm probably not. I try to understand the needs and wants of potential clients, and my job is to listen and see how I can help them." He hadn't been shooting the breeze at all, but rather had been asking probing questions in a nice, informal way. He recognized that the point of the job was to make customers' lives easier, and he could do that if he could learn whether the program would be a benefit to them. He explained to me that he didn't have a design background and realized early in his stint with our company that he didn't need one. He was right. Sales guys should understand what will benefit the customer, and have the knowledge to impart that to their clients.

In our company most of the team came from a building or architectural background. John, however, didn't—same as me—and as soon as I realized that, I saw it as a weakness that we both shared. Rather than trying to address that lack of experience by immersing himself in the program, though, he had developed a system where he understood the market, his leads, and their requirements. He was no slouch at design, don't get me wrong, but if the questions got too complicated he reached out to our technical staff. I learned from that and began to focus more on my understanding of types of architecture in my specific territories, and local design and building requirements. I learned everything I could about the solutions and abilities of our program, but began to worry less about every nuance in an incredibly-involved software. If I ever got trapped in a design demonstration and was unable to quickly address a complex aspect of the program, I learned it was OK to tell the customer I didn't know. Simply enough, I'd find out and get back to them. To the credit of those professionals, I can't think of any time ever that a potential customer had a problem with that answer.

The important thing to me, as a salesman, was to be able to address the concerns of our clients, and I could best do that by understanding exactly what they needed from a design program. That's what I was good at. I didn't need to be able to master every aspect of our program, and it was a relief when I admitted that to myself. But we focus on our deficiencies so much that we tend to overlook our strengths. It's impossible to know everything, and the only true way to fail is by not recognizing that you always have room to learn and grow. In time I became a much better salesman simply by focusing more on the customer than the program. I had the ability to listen, and gained true empathy toward the professional requirements of potential clients. I should also note that the sales manager that hired me was the same one who had earlier brought on board our California representative. I later asked him why he would hire salesmen for a design program who really didn't know that much about building. He answered that he had developed the ability to recognize strengths in people and knew enough to make the positives of attitude and intelligence outweigh any lack of design knowledge—design being something that he could teach. As it turns out, my trip to California was a designed learning experience and was as beneficial as my boss had imagined it would be. Even today, when I pick up the phone or read an email my first thought is how can I help these people. While I still acknowledge my weaknesses, I will never give in to them. Neither should you.

*****

The Battle of Cowpens — 1781

"You don't hurt 'em if you don't hit 'em."
Lt. General Lewis "Chesty" Puller

When your back is against the wall you must explore every option, and sometimes that takes you to a place that calls upon every resource you have. As a salesman of an architectural design program, I spoke with countless builders who were facing the reality that they were aging out of their ability to climb a roof or frame a house. Many wanted to transition their knowledge of building into the design aspect of the industry, but had concerns about their capacity to draw blueprints on a computer. They simply needed to realize that they already had the talent and the desire, and though it might not have been obvious to them at first, the ability. They knew the industry, the architecture, and the techniques. Their lack of design experience was not the weakness they thought. I submit that their lack of design experience was just a strength that hadn't been tested. We see the same thing in military history, and especially through the eyes of "green" or untrained troops. The typical young soldier fears "seeing the elephant" for the first time, and he wonders whether he's ready. One historic battle really stands out for me as an example of an army that fully utilized both its strengths and weaknesses, and is a story I want you to remember anytime that you begin to underestimate yourself.

***

The young colonel was pleased with himself. As he considered the upcoming battle he must have smiled at the thought that this had been more like a fox hunt than an effort in putting down a rebellion. The chase had gone for miles and days, but his quarry had done what a fox would so often do—become trapped. Though there would be a fight, the end was inevitable. His men were tired, as they had been marching since hours before dawn in this final pursuit. They were hungry and weak, as well; rations had been minimal while chasing their foe. But it would soon be over, and there was no doubt as to what the outcome would be. There was a certain luxury in commanding troops of one of the best armies on the face of the planet, and the colonel, no stranger to success, had an even greater advantage. He was facing an army largely consisting of militia. The militia was usually undisciplined, poorly equipped, and often prone to running as soon as they saw the bayonet. As if things couldn't get better, his opponent had made a tactical mistake by stopping with his back against a rain-swollen river, effectively cutting off any method of escape. Yes, it might have been more prudent to wait and prepare for a proper assault. But why? Lieutenant Colonel Banastre Tarleton hastily sent dragoons riding forward as he moved his men into their standard deployment. From the woods he brought into line his two "grasshopper" cannons and quickly ordered the infantry to advance. The American rebels at Cowpens were inferior, and he would soon teach them the lesson that many of their countrymen had already learned: that rabble could never stand against a premiere British force. It was all over but the shooting.

It was January of 1781, and the American Revolution was in its fifth year. For the British, the northern battles had been a series of small victories, stalemates, and even severe failures, such as at Saratoga. There was pressure from king and country to get this thing wrapped up once and for all. With their Southern Campaign the British were hoping to bring the southern colonies back under their firm control, believing them more loyal than the northern colonies. Once that was done, they could then again focus on the north. Some suggested a pincer movement, forcing the rebels into the middle colonies. Others simply suggested writing off the North altogether; it seemed to be the core of the treason and didn't have nearly the strategic and economic value of the South. If there had to be a choice for a prize, let it be Charleston, Savannah, or Wilmington.

Lieutenant Colonel Banastre Tarleton had made a name for himself as commander of the British Legion, and was especially popular for his role in the victory at Camden. To the British and Loyalists, he was a bright and shining star, still in his mid-twenties, and the epitome of British success. But to the patriots—the rebels—he was branded as an extreme villain. In fact, due to his supposed massacre at the Battle of the Waxhaws, the unwillingness to take prisoners was sometimes called "Tarleton's Quarter."

The American forces were commanded by General Daniel Morgan, nicknamed "The Old Wagoneer" for his role as a civilian teamster during the French and Indian War. In the following years, Morgan had become an experienced soldier, serving as one of the first volunteers after Lexington and Concord and gaining the rank of colonel after the failed American assault upon Quebec. An interesting character in his own right, he had the experience to anticipate his enemy's movements, the understanding of his own troop's strengths (and weaknesses), and the awareness to utilize every resource to his own advantage. He had played a large part in the American victory at Saratoga, and at Cowpens he would demonstrate a daring and audacity seldom seen in the American Revolution.

The Cowpens had long been a well-known spot in the backwoods of South Carolina. As one might expect from its name, it was a good grazing area for cattle. But the location had recently become better known as the place where thousands of backwoodsmen had gathered the previous October before marching off to fight Major Patrick Ferguson and his Loyalists at the Battle of Kings Mountain. Small groups of men would be arriving throughout the night, bolstering the ranks of Morgan's men, and, out of necessity, he needed a landmark they could easily find. The Cowpens was a grassy field dotted with trees and situated on a bit of an incline. The rise was a gradual slope with a slight valley further up, then continuing upwards to the low ridgeline.

Morgan recognized, as had Tarleton, the tendency of Patriot militia to break and run under pressure. He needed to find a way to use them in combination with his professionally trained soldiers—the Continental troops. He anticipated that Tarleton, in a rush, would deploy his Redcoats in a traditional manner. Therefore, Morgan established his troops in three battle lines with little regard for his flanks. His first line of engagement was to be his sharpshooters, and their sole job was to disrupt the approaching British, understanding that targeting officers would certainly do that. Behind the sharpshooters, at perhaps 150 yards, was the militia. All that was asked of them were two musket volleys at the approaching British. After those shots they were to run for protection behind the Continentals and the ridgeline. It was a bold concept, but Morgan felt that was the most he could expect from the militia, which were the majority of his troops. Totally unanticipated by Tarleton and his men, this understanding would prove to be a major difference in the battle.

The opening moments were as classic as a battle scene from a Shakespeare play. The Patriots stood and waited, the crisp morning air as pure as ever. At the crest of the hill the Continental line stood smartly in their tricorn hats, blue coats, and white breeches and stockings. Armed with British Land Pattern muskets (the Brown Bess) they would match with their enemy, who were carrying the same type arms. Below them the scene was different and shifting. There was the militia clad in their hunting shirts and buckskin outfits, carrying their familiar Kentucky Rifles. Sprinkled throughout was a bit of civilian and a hodgepodge of homespun. These men were guaranteed to hit their intended targets, and they knew they could make their two shots sting.

The British emerged from the forest and began to assemble, and the Americans could finally see their pursuers. Colonel Tarleton's British Legion was outfitted in an attractive green, as was he. His artillerymen manning those grasshoppers, the small brass cannons, wore their traditional blue uniforms. It would be muskets and bayonets, with the cannons barking and men cheering. To the center of the line went the infantry, wearing their long-established redcoats, with millinery ranging from bearskin hats to the same fashionable tricorns as the Continental soldiers. As with their opponents, the British could see their breath on this bitterly cold day, and many must have wondered whether they were exhaling their last. For the survivors it would someday be a glorious story to regale their spellbound grandchildren.

Fifes played and drums beat their instruction as the battle began in earnest for the British. Their infantry stepped forward and, protected by mounted Dragoons on both flanks, moved up the incline toward the Patriots. When the British infantry came into range of the American guns, the Patriot sharpshooters completed their goal, targeting Tarleton's officers. Mission completed, they fell back toward the line of militia. The British line had been hit by their fire and disrupted, but continued with its steady movement up the slight slope. Their tactic of the day was a massed concentration of musket fire, then a bayonet attack into any breach that had been created. But they needed to get closer to the Americans for that tactic to be effective. As Morgan had hoped, most of his militiamen were also able to fire a couple of shots at the oncoming Redcoats, before running to their left behind the safety of the hill and their Continental compatriots.

The British came forward, undaunted, as would be expected of a professional army. Both sides fired volley after volley and the chaos and din of battle was overwhelming and confusing. As the British Dragoons began to gallop into the Patriot lines, the American cavalry, under command of Colonel William Washington, came bursting from cover. In response, Tarleton deployed his Scotsmen, who had been held in reserve. They slammed into the Patriot right flank and, among the cacophony of their bagpipes, their rallying shouts, and incessant musket fire, the Patriots began to withdraw. But Morgan, refusing to accept that his men would be turned so easily, rode into the melee to rally the troops. Hearing their commander's shouts of encouragement and witnessing his bravery and defiance, the Americans turned and fired, halting the charging British with the unexpected assault. The Redcoats staggered back and the Patriots experienced a rush of exuberance. Bayonets fixed, the Americans trotted down the hill, rapidly becoming a wave of destruction against the dispersing British. The rout was on.

The British soldiers reacted in several ways. Many officers had been killed by the targeted shots of the sharpshooters and militia, and the resulting lack of leadership combined with exhaustion and uncertainty to instill a confusion into the British. Several men just sat down and gave up, regardless of injury, while others fled back down the hill. Some cavalry continued to fight, understanding their proper role as the breakdown began, while others refused orders to be sent into the fray. The artillerymen manned their guns until the end and their valor resulted in their complete annihilation. The British were almost in a situation of complete destruction. Colonel Tarleton, himself, ended up in a personal fight with Colonel Washington before galloping from the field with the remainder of his disoriented army. The battle was over by 8:00 AM, and though it had lasted little more than an hour, the result changed the complexion of the entire war. Against the odds, Morgan's innovative planning and approach won this battle. Cornwallis was devastated by the results and, a year later, he was at Yorktown surrendering his army to General George Washington.

Many historians consider Morgan's unorthodox deployment and use of the militia—so often unreliable—as the most innovative use of troops during the American Revolution. In fact, those were the days when soldiers usually just lined up, marched forward, took a shot at the enemy, and repeat. Fighting with that traditional method gave the advantage to the troops who were professionally trained. Make no mistake: Banastre Tarleton was a very capable officer and proved himself well in other battles. To win this fight, Morgan needed his militia and his professional Continental soldiers. Even that would not have been enough had he used them in the typical "fire-and-march" method. He knew that he had to do something beyond the same-old, same-old, which was almost a guaranteed loss against properly trained, disciplined troops.

That "something" was that he recognized his militia as an asset, even if a limited one. He also understood that the British felt that the American militia would never be able to stand in the face of a professional army. To them the militia was a disorderly group that would always break and run. Morgan knew that he could probably rely on his volunteers to fire a couple of shots, but he also knew that when they followed his orders to retreat to the rear, the British would perceive that as the beginning of a rout. That's exactly what happened, and in what was likely a success beyond his wildest hopes, those backcountry men were put into play in the trouncing of the British at Cowpens. As an aside, even with General Morgan's innovations, Tarleton's Legion still might have won the battle. But Colonel Tarleton "played the game" the way he always had, and by the time he recognized what was happening, it was too late. He didn't consider his own weakness—underestimating his opponent—and he blindly rushed into disaster.

As Daniel Morgan did with his maligned militia, you must consider every attribute you have as a potential advantage. Most of us are good at understanding our strengths, and the honest among us can understand our so-called weaknesses. But many of us never take advantage of opportunities, even those we see, because we don't understand that we're capable. Or, just as likely, because we're afraid. We tend to avoid and fear the unfamiliar, even when we must know it's an irrational fear. Morgan's tactics at Cowpens were beyond unconventional, and there's no doubt that he recognized the gamble he put into play with such unprecedented tactics.

Weaknesses can be developed into strengths in many cases, and they can always be improved. Likewise, it's important to never neglect the strengths that have made you a success. Play to your strengths, but always remember that you have many abilities and alternatives, and none of them should ever be overlooked or discounted.

4

LEARN FROM YOUR MISTAKES: THE BATTLE OF HASTINGS

"By seeking and blundering we learn."
Johann Wolfgang von Goethe

There's an expression that experience is the best teacher, and I know that to be true. We all make mistakes, and undoubtedly the biggest ones stick with us forever. You often hear people say, "Well, I'll never make that mistake again." And they don't, because they learned.

I grew up on a small family farm. That meant hard work and, sometimes, hard lessons. Our farm was a typical one for that time in Tennessee, set alongside the Cumberland River with a few acres of burley tobacco and maybe 50 head of cattle. We used some of our acreage for grazing and some for hay, with the opportunity to change crops when it was time to rotate. The two main cash crops we had when I was a kid were tobacco and corn. My father and grandfather were experts on both those crops, and I believed they must have known everything there was to know about agriculture. They knew how to combat the diseases, the harmful insects, the droughts, and, to a certain extent, the floods. But in the late 1960s they were struck by an enemy they couldn't combat: the United States government.

The U.S. Corps of Engineers had decided to place a dam on the Cumberland River. The result would be a much wider river, with flooding of the bottomland. That would result in some of our property being covered by water, especially with the government taking an excess as a buffer against future floods. There, as you guessed, was our primary corn production. It was time to evaluate which direction the family farm would go. Soon after the taking of our property, there were a couple of events that sent our farm in a different direction. First, my grandfather passed away, and with him went a world of experience, as well as a man who could always be counted on to be in the field when the sun came up. At the same time—and here comes the irony—the government was paying people to not grow corn. Yes, a farmer could draw a check for acreage diversion, which is the fancy term for getting paid to not do something. My dad, being a smart young man, decided to take them up on that offer. But he did have a family and an urge to work, so he had to do something.

Enter soybeans. Food requirements were up in many places around the world, and soybeans were a major commodity, especially in the Soviet Union. After a lot of research, my dad determined that soybeans were the best option for him. First, it was a type of production that could be primarily, if not wholly, handled by one man on a small farm. Second, others in the area were beginning to raise the crop, so the volume was enough to facilitate the local creation of the needed infrastructure. Plainly, he needed a place to sell soybeans, and that now existed nearby, even though it had not just a few years earlier. Dad bought a used combine with a head that would harvest his soybeans and an old 1957 International Harvester two-ton flatbed truck that would haul his crop. It was a major step, but he had learned everything he could about the growing and production of soybeans. My dad has a great expression he uses after he's studied something for too long: "All right, boys. Let's do something, even if it's wrong." And off he went to be the best new soybean farmer in middle Tennessee.

Dad made sure the ground was properly fertilized for legumes; he watched as the weather cooperated, and with a lot of hard work he came up with a great bean yield. By his reckoning, his bushels-per-acre ratio was wonderful, much better than expected. The old combine worked like a charm, and the truck, though not fast at all, was able to make the winding, 30-mile trip to Smithville to offload the crop. Time and time again it did that, with my dad being paid the daily market price for his beans. On one of his trips, another farmer was unloading his crop and stepped over to ask my dad what price per bushel he was getting that day. My dad told him and then asked why he didn't just check his own ticket to see. The other farmer replied that he had already sold his soybeans on the futures market at a higher price, he thought, than they were bringing that day. The concept was familiar, like something you'd hear at the end of a local radio station's farm report, but nothing Dad knew anything about. He got a five-minute lesson that day from the other farmer, then set himself to learning everything he possibly could about the futures market. He talked to every other soybean farmer he could, he consulted the county agricultural agent, and he read the newspapers to get a better grip on the commodities markets. By the time the next year rolled around my dad was an expert on soybean production and supply, worldwide markets, potential weather-related crop failures, and especially the Soviet outlook that year. Beyond that, he had to accurately gauge what his production would be, because the sale of futures needed to be as close as possible to final output without promising more than could be delivered.

Dad had a selling price in mind that he felt would eventually crop up (pun intended), and he called an automated phone system every day, just waiting and hoping that the bid would get to the price level he thought it should be. I remember sitting there one afternoon, watching what had become a routine for the past few weeks, when he suddenly said, "That's it." He immediately went through a process and locked in the full farm production with that one bid. We were never sure whether he hit the absolute top of the market, but it must have been very close, and was a much better price than the random days of fall would have brought.

My dad had earlier made a rookie mistake. He's a great farmer, and, when he transitioned from corn to soybeans, he learned everything he could about the best soil for the new crop, as well as proper drainage and all the challenges that come with a no-till plant that could enhance erosion. He learned the best herbicides, when to harvest, the least expensive way to haul his crop, and any number of things that helped lead to success. He made a mistake, but it was more an error of omission, and he immediately and effectively addressed it. He recognized that there was a better way to sell and optimized that understanding. There is a tremendous amount of good that comes from recognizing mistakes, especially those we make ourselves, and I always ask myself when I blunder, as my dad did: "What can I learn from that?" The only bad lesson is the one from which we learn nothing.

*****

The Battle of Hastings — 1066

"Success does not consist in never making mistakes, but in never making the same one a second time."
George Bernard Shaw

To err is human, goes the saying, and we all have made mistakes. The key to becoming a success in this world is to accept the mistakes you make as learning opportunities and to do your best never to repeat them. Mark Twain said that there are no mistakes in life, only lessons to be learned. The key is to be sure that you learn that lesson the first time you have the chance. The history of western civilization was turned on its side almost 1,000 years ago when soldiers made a critical mistake in the midst of battle, then made the same mistake again. Obviously, there isn't a lesson of success that might be learned from them, but I do have a bit of a warning—a second chance doesn't always happen.

***

Duke William was pleased. He had organized one of the most

successful amphibious operations of all time, and his invading force had met practically no resistance at its landing. Perhaps that was as it should have been. He believed that his claim to the throne was valid, and surely God would have wanted to intervene on behalf of such a just cause. Yet he also had to consider that he was the second usurper to have recently crossed over from the continent, hoping to take the throne. The Scandinavians had also felt they had a claim, but they had been defeated by King Harold II, soundly, and just days earlier. The Viking incursion, though, had forced the king to use precious men and resources. At that earlier battle it had been brother against brother, with all the hatred and violence that usually accompanies such fratricide. But the king had prevailed, and, satisfied that he had the strength needed for this latest invader, force-marched south. He could have waited for reinforcements or to rest his men, but decided the need for a quick victory was more important. He was confident as he chose his spot for battle, and his opponent was glad for nothing more than the opportunity to fight. English King Harold Godwinson stood ready to meet the latest foe that would challenge his authority. That opponent, the Duke of Normandy, promised God that, should he be victorious that day, he would build an abbey in remembrance of the men who fell. Two armies faced each other in southern England, and history was in the balance, as perhaps it had never been before.

It was October of 1066, and because of the recent death of the King of England, there were three distinct and valid claims to the throne. King Edward the Confessor had, on his deathbed, promised the throne to Harold Godwinson, an English royal. Harold strongly desired the throne and took the power as given to him. He faced a problem, though, in that he had earlier promised his support to a cousin of the recently deceased king. William, Duke of Normandy, was a cousin of Edward the Confessor and had previously gained the pledge of Harold. There was little doubt that Harold, as Earl of Wessex, had made such an oath, but the pledge had been largely coerced during a time of captivity, and he felt no obligation to keep it. He reckoned that he deserved the kingdom much more than the illegitimate William, the Norman pretender, and would fight any man to prove his right to the throne.

King Harold knew that he would have a fight in 1066, and he waited to see from where it would first come. In a bit of irony, before he could confront the enemy from Normandy, he had to fight his exiled brother, Tostig, and the Vikings. That Battle of Stamford Bridge was a bloody affair, but one in which the English army killed Tostig, as well as King Harald of Norway and most of the Norwegians who had taken York. The defeat of the Vikings had been made easier because of Harold's quick deployment from the south of England, north to Yorkshire. The arrival of the English army on the battlefield, just a few miles from York, had been a complete surprise to the invaders.

Just three days after the battle of Stamford Bridge, William, Duke of Normandy, successfully landed an even larger invasion force on the southern coast of England. King Harold had to return south immediately. Within three weeks, incredibly, Harold and his men were a few miles northwest of the coastal town of Hastings, waiting on William.

The English army consisted primarily of infantry, and would possibly be smaller than that of the Norman invaders. Harold had left some of his better soldiers in the north, including most of his archers, but rather than wait on larger numbers of reinforcements from other parts of his kingdom, he had quickly regrouped in London and decided to go ahead and make a fight of it. Surprise had worked against his first challenger and might be just what he needed for his second.

For his part, Duke William had hastily erected a fort at a small coastal town called Pevensey, and would not have been surprised that Harold and his men were attempting to make a quick challenge to his occupation. In fact, it was to the benefit of the invading Normans to decide the matter as expeditiously as possible. Every hour meant the opportunity for more English to join their king, and William's stalled army of thousands would soon lay bare the country of food and supplies. His options were clear. He could advance to London and the countryside, but that would extend his supply lines and leave him more vulnerable to attack. He could return to his ships, but that would be worse than defeat at this point. His final option was to show fight, and so it would be.

King Harold used great military reasoning in choosing the specific hilltop on which to make his stand, noting that the location would serve as an effective barrier between the Normans and the route toward London and the interior of the country. Senlac Hill would prove to be the perfect spot, with trees and undergrowth complementing the steep grades on both his army's right and left flanks. Those geographic and natural features would make it impossible for the Normans to advance from any direction other than directly forward. Even better, the ground at the bottom of the hill was wet and soggy, making it more difficult for the maneuver of cavalry. Harold's army consisted of about 8,000 men. Of those, about half were professional soldiers fighting explicitly for the king and his brothers, Leofwine and

Gyrth. The balance of his army consisted of landowners and fyrds, which were part-time fighters and peasants. The English style of fighting was on foot, and though many had arrived by horse, they would dismount for the fight. Harold's army was large enough to completely cover the crest of the hill, and he deployed his troops from west to east, having his professional soldiers form a shield wall with the peasants behind them.

The professional soldiers of the Saxon English wore knee-length shirts of mail and metal helmets with protection extending to cover the nose. Further armament came in the form of two types of shields: round and kite. Kite shields were shaped to give protection along the height of the man, yet allowing the opportunity to deliver crushing blows with a sword. Round shields were also common at that time, especially among the Danes, and many of the English had likely picked up Norse shields at Stamford Bridge, especially if theirs had been broken there. These were the days before heraldry, but there would have been a variety of colors and designs among their shields. The King's bodyguards and other professional soldiers carried a variety of weapons including the Danish Axe, which was a two-handed axe with a handle sometimes extending to five feet in length. The Danish Axe had the capacity of splitting a horse's head and, as the saying went, opening a man from grin to groin. Along with the axe, most soldiers would have carried a sword, and possibly a spear. The peasants were not, as one would expect, as well-armed and equipped. Their weapons ranged from swords to mere farming implements, and their clothing varied from simple cloth, to leather, to the occasional mail. The English were warriors with long hair and beards, contrasting with the clean-cut Normans. Harold and his bodyguard took their position at the top of the hill, in the center. His location was marked by his famous Fighting Man banner, adorned with gold and precious stones, and his Standard of Wessex, which was a red and gold windsock-type device emblazoned with a dragon.

The Normans approached the English lines on horseback, and many of them would fight as cavalry. William deployed his Bretons from Maine and Anjou to the west, crossing in front of the Saxons, who were assembled at the hilltop. The Franco-Flemish would deploy to his right, and his own Normans would take the center. William's men on the field were a professional army consisting of 3,000 infantry, 2,000 cavalry, and 800 archers. Most were garbed in the same style of chain mail as their opponents, yet primarily armed with swords and spears, with a steady preference toward the kite shield. A variety of banners flew among the invaders, but of specific importance that day was a papal banner signifying that the pope was supportive of Duke William and his quest. As with his adversary, William also had family on the field, his half-brothers Bishop Odo and Robert.

The English stood as one on the hilltop, banging their swords against shields, shouting their versions of "Holy Cross" and "God Almighty." Meanwhile, Duke William rode to the front of his lines, readying his mind for the assault that he must make. As his troops prepared themselves, his juggler tossed swords and recited the epic poem *Song of Roland*, the story of a hero who fought with Charlemagne. The juggler, perhaps in bravery or perhaps by accident, rode his horse into the English lines and became the first casualty of the Battle of Hastings.

Duke William knew that he had to break the English shield wall above him, and his best chance was to use his archers and then exploit any openings that occurred. His archers lofted their arrows into the air, but many went over the heads of the Saxons because of the slope of the hill, while others were stopped by their shields. The English had come south so quickly from Stamford Bridge that they had left most of their own archers along the way. While the English would have wanted their archers alongside them, at least their absence meant that the Normans would not be able to reuse any arrows they might have shot in return. Recognizing that the shield wall still stood as it had at the beginning of the battle, William sent forward his infantry. They would advance, and the cavalry would wait to exploit any gaps that they opened. On the Norman left flank the battle became very heated. The English there began to gain an advantage, causing the Norman invaders on that side of the line to flee down the hill. Disregarding their previous instruction, many English charged down the hill after their scurrying enemy. That was a mistake as it broke their shield wall and exposed their own right flank. Perhaps it was the excitement of realizing the battle might be won, or perhaps it was because the peasants were thinking of the loot they might gain. Regardless, it was a mistake. Many of them would soon be surrounded and lose their own lives. The English were able to reform the shield wall on their right flank, though, and their defense was once again in order.

The English position remained a strong one, and the battle continued for hours. The Norman forces were exhausting themselves with continued assaults up the hill. Battles in the medieval period were generally short because men and horses depleted their energy so quickly. Yet this one continued on and on, to the point that men took rest breaks and even stopped to eat. But William's options were limited, and it was to his advantage to continue the fight. He sent both infantry and cavalry up the hill time and again, but their efforts were practically useless. As they approached the crest and the shield wall, the English threw knives, stones, swords, and anything else they had which might cause damage or death. As the cavalry approached the English lines, they had to wheel their horses to the left to strike with their swords, as most men were right-handed. But this required maneuver exposed their horses' flanks to the long reach of the Danish axes. After hours of battle, the shield wall had become reinforced with the dead bodies of men and horses. Duke William realized that his chance of victory was slipping away, and he needed some type of advantage.

William had noticed the previous encounter on his left flank, the one in which his men ran, and decided that might be an opportunity. In the previous encounter, both sides had made mistakes: the Normans by running, and the English by giving chase. William instructed his men on the left flank to show fight as they had previously. But, at a prearranged time, they were to flee down the hill as they had before, hopefully drawing the undisciplined English after them. It was a simple trick, but it worked, and as the English right flank broke to chase the Normans, William's cavalry was ready to sweep up the shield wall from the side. It was likely around this time that King Harold's brothers were killed, and with the loss of their guidance, the exhausted English were practically doomed against an organized cavalry assault. King Harold was an experienced soldier and was willing to carry the fight, but was struck in the eye by an arrow and then killed by a group of Norman cavalry who had broken through the crumbling lines. The King's bodyguard kept fighting, as did a considerable number of his professional soldiers who had sworn to do so, but many others fled from the field. The Norman victory was complete.

Some Normans gave chase to those fleeing, but night was approaching in that unfamiliar country, and they regretted that decision. A good number of the retreating English had turned back to cover the exodus and were more than happy to eliminate several of the Normans who had the audacity to come after them. The survivors decided that discretion was the better part of valor and rode back to the battlefield and their victorious army. The English did put up a rebellion for a few years, but hindsight showed Hastings as the deciding battle. A foreign army had invaded and occupied England for the last time in history, and the name William the Conqueror would be etched into its long line of kings.

In not waiting for rest or reinforcements, the biggest mistake of all was Harold's. Had he delayed for just a few days, his archers could have arrived and his flanks would have been protected. His army had not been in any danger, and reinforcements from throughout the kingdom would have continued to arrive. The situation on the right flank at Hastings is practically inexcusable and can be attributed to inexperience and the excitement of battle. Every soldier in that shield wall knew that it must be maintained at all costs. Yet they failed, not in numbers or effort, but by lack of discipline.

Most school children can quote the old saying: "Fool me once, shame on you. Fool me twice, shame on me." But deception to gain an advantage can be a powerful tool, as deadly a weapon as a sword or axe. The Anglo-Saxons at Hastings were tricked into an egregious mistake and never had the opportunity to learn from it. They were effectively destroyed. Luckily, for most of us, we're able to take the stings of our mistakes and turn those into perfect learning experiences. In fact, we're usually the only ones who cheat ourselves, when time and again we fail to learn from our blunders. Accept setbacks as natural learning opportunities, then do your best to never repeat them. Honestly learn from your mistakes.

5

KEEP YOUR OPTIONS OPEN: THE BATTLE OF ALESIA

"Luck is what happens when preparation meets opportunity."
Seneca

I have a Bachelor of Science degree in Finance from the University of Tennessee, and that diploma reflects a lot of work. It also reflects a lot of time, anguish, and second-guessing. That's because I wanted to major in history or English, or almost anything else that didn't involve numbers. As a high school junior, I wasn't sure that I wanted to go to college and hadn't given it a lot of thought or planning. The thought of just staying on the farm had an appeal, and I even considered becoming a truck driver. Movies such as *Smokey and the Bandit* and *Every*

Which Way but Loose and TV shows like *BJ and the Bear* and *The Dukes of Hazzard* were all the rage. That could be me, pulling a load of who-knows-what to who-knows-where, in my custom-painted Kenworth big rig. Throw in a couple of beautiful women escaping the clutches of a corrupt sheriff, maybe even a pet chimpanzee riding shotgun, and I'd have the perfect world after high school.

As if on cue, my parents entered the discussion and weren't too thrilled with my idea of skipping college for truck driving school. To be clear, my parents felt that truck driving and farming were both honorable professions. It was simply that neither of them had finished college, and they felt that the lack of a degree had limited their options. My mom, in fact, held a high-level job in governmental finance. But she faced artificial limits only because she didn't have the degree required for certain federal positions. That great job had taken her years to obtain and required more effort than most people would ever have given. She reminded me of the classes she took in her 30s, learning things such as shorthand and accounting, and asked me to consider at least one year of college. Plainly, she worried that I would be limiting myself if I didn't explore alternatives—options that she felt certain I'd someday want. Her argument was solid, and within a few days I was talking with the high school guidance counselor.

Mrs. Pharris was my guidance counselor and a lady I had known since childhood. Her advice to me was blunt. It was her opinion that I could do almost anything, but that I should major in something that would give me the ability to remain flexible as to profession. Her concern was that my preferred history and English would limit me to becoming a teacher or a librarian. Those were fine aspirations, she noted, but were too limiting for a young man who, just a week earlier, wasn't sure whether he wanted to teach Eudora Welty or drive an eighteen-wheeler across the country. After a good discussion, and some wailing and gnashing of teeth, we decided that I would major in finance, but that I could combine that with a heavy emphasis on English. Her thinking was that I'd enjoy finance, but that I needed to stay flexible in the event of a changed mind after enrollment. Her best advice to me was to always have options and to never find myself in a situation from which I couldn't make at least a lateral move.

Looking back, it's obvious that I wasn't ready for college. I took a variety of classes that interested me, and didn't show the focus that I needed. I didn't particularly enjoy accounting classes—I found them boring—and my grades reflected that. I even dropped out of school for a year to "find myself," and to decide whether college was the answer for me. A daytime job as a taxpayer service representative with the Internal Revenue Service, combined with a few months of loading night-shift trucks at United Parcel Service, turned out to be plenty of "finding myself." I went back to school and promptly earned that finance degree that had once seemed almost unattainable.

In the professional world I've held various jobs, as opportunities and interests have arisen. My philosophy has always been to learn everything I can at a job, because that's where you find opportunity. I have been manager and peon, finding challenges and benefits in all roles. My last job as an accountant was overseeing the finances of a software development company. The software was an incredible program, aimed at home builders, and was nothing in which I had any relevant experience. Still, I figured that if I were to be employed by a software company, I needed to know about the program. With the boss's permission,

I took a copy home to work with and designed a little project for my own home. I wasn't an expert, but I wasn't half-bad.

A couple months later the company had a situation where they needed some extra help on the phones during the end-of-the year rush, and I was asked if I could pitch in to answer sales calls. I was a little apprehensive. But even though I had never done pure sales, I found the job exciting. The most exhilarating thing I had done professionally in the past couple years was simultaneously fielding audits from the Internal Revenue Service and Revenue Canada. My books were perfect, the audits ended with a whimper, and I was ready for something else. The bit of experience I gained that December was great for me, and when a full-time sales job became available, I was given the first option at it. I took it, and it was a great transition for me, both professionally and financially. I never saw myself as just an accountant; I saw myself as a man with options. My boss had given me the opportunity, but he would never have been able to do that had I remained static and stagnant—seeing myself in just that one role.

Opportunity is everywhere, and you owe it to yourself to learn and experience as much as you can, because you need to be ready when the possibility of something you desire presents itself. Take the initiative, continue learning, consider all options, and never limit yourself.

*****

The Battle of Alesia — 52 BC

"It's easier to stay out than get out."
Mark Twain

Too many times in life we allow fear of failure, or even minor setbacks, to paralyze us. But the best thing we can do is to confront our fears, face the battle before us, and do something to effect a change for the better. In history, especially on the battlefield, we often see brave men suffer from hesitancy and uncertainty, and they seem frozen and unable to follow their own best judgment. I think most of us can relate to that feeling. I certainly do. There's a quote by Teddy Roosevelt that I've always liked: "In any moment of decision, the best thing you can do is the right thing, and the worst thing you can do is nothing." The right thing is usually as simple as saying, "I can do this," neglecting your irrational fear, and stepping forward to the challenge.

***

The Roman governor stood in his tower watching the battle unfold, and the results were becoming disastrous. This attack had been expected, but with miles of wall to defend, and against such large numbers, there had been no way to prepare completely. The air was filled with arrows and stones, from without and from within, and the screams of dying men and horses punctuated the realization that this was it—this was his last opportunity at success in this foreign land. The Gauls within the enclosure were doing everything they could to accomplish a breakout of the trap, and the 200,000 men who had come to their rescue were making an assault for the ages, with the full intent of breaching the palisade before them. The break had happened, and the odds against the governor had never been greater. In fact, his army was down to what was practically its last man. As a military genius, he could see that he was to be that last man, and as a strong believer in luck, he would do all in his power to assist that condition. He turned to a nearby centurion and nodded, calling up the last four cohorts of his army. He was their governor, he was their general, and he was their comrade-in-arms. He placed his helmet upon his head, girded and flung his crimson cloak around his shoulders, then drew the sword that must strike victory on this day. His men recognized the distinctive red cloak as he strode into the fray and realized that their desperation was also his. It had all been a gamble, and this would be his last throw of the dice. Julius Caesar was never hesitant to play against his luck, and his faith in himself and his men was all that mattered now. His men cheered with a renewed energy as he was recognized, and the push forward began. How could the Gauls defeat them when Caesar himself had joined the battle?

It was 52 BC, and the Gallic Wars had been ongoing for six years. While the Rhine River had been viewed as a natural barrier between Rome and the Gauls, many Romans felt that the threat should be eliminated. Likewise, many also saw a conquered Gaul as a good way to become wealthy. Among these was Julius Caesar, who, as governor, had the most to gain. Many Gallic tribes had been allies to Rome, though sometimes reluctantly, but things had changed. While there had always been a hint of rebellion among these tribes, the Romans usually had little trouble stamping out the fires, as it were. The tribes of Gaul had long seen themselves as fiercely independent, and their inability to work together was sometimes as defeating as their Roman invaders.

As so often happens in history, an invaded and occupied people will eventually rise. In Gaul it had begun with an assortment of tribes, some previously friendly to Rome, and others not at all.

The Gauls were experienced warriors with a reputation as being ferocious in battle. Larger than the Romans, they wore wild hair, colorful and patterned pants and shirts, drawstring shoes, and beautiful silver and golden neck rings called torcs. With swords, shields, and horses, they had equipped themselves to function well as infantry and cavalry. They had the advantage in numbers, and their cities were often walled and resistant to any attack. What these independent tribes lacked, though, was leadership beyond their individual communities. Into this gap stepped Vercingetorix, a young noble intent on carrying forward the rebellious nature of his ancestry. Vercingetorix recognized that the Romans were experienced troops with discipline, teamwork, and an understanding of warfare beyond anything the Gauls had, especially when operating in large numbers. His first attempts at directly engaging the Romans in battle had not been successful, and he realized that he needed another strategy.

What the Romans really lacked was an effective supply system. They had to rely on their few Gallic allies and their own wits for food and provisions, and that reliance was a weakness on which the Gauls could prey. Plainly, the hungry invaders would be susceptible to being picked off one by one and little by little. To be successful at starving the Roman legions, though, Vercingetorix had to convince the independent tribes to destroy their own crops and to abandon their cities, in effect betting that the Romans would starve before his own people would. That was a hard choice, but most felt that it was worth it to rid themselves of the invader.

But there would surely be holdouts, and most notably among those were the 40,000 inhabitants of Avaricum. Their walled city was well-constructed in the typical Gaulish style of earth and timbers, which would stand against fire and battering ram—practically impenetrable. Further, it had an incredible natural defense, being virtually surrounded by rivers. The city was also a tribal capital, which made it even more difficult to participate in the "scorched earth" policy that the Gauls were using against the Romans.

For his part, Julius Caesar saw Avaricum as an opportunity. Though the rivers and marshes were obstacles, they only helped him focus on what had to be his point of siege, his point of attack. Ever the strategist, Caesar maintained an army that was part soldier and part engineer. His legionaries were familiar with digging ditches, building camps, and any number of mundane tasks that have always been the bane of a soldier. Their options were limited but clear. If they couldn't go through, then they'd just go over. Protected by mobile sheds, they set about moving earth to create ramps up to the walls of the city. With incredible speed, considering the task before them, they constructed siege towers that could be rolled up the ramps.

The abilities of the Romans were not lost on the Gauls. They understood the dangers implicit in merely remaining behind their walls and would venture out to destroy the Roman defenses, or would send fire over the walls to stop the progress of their siege works. Vercingetorix and his men were outside the city and doing their best to thwart Caesar's progress. But discipline and engineering won out, and on a blustery night the siege towers were rolled forward, and the walls were overcome.

Caesar made the Gauls pay for their insolence. Almost all the 40,000 citizens of Avaricum were put to the sword, and the city was sacked. Caesar's rationale was that such a massacre would be a lesson to the resistance, and he certainly hoped for a quick submission throughout the country. Rather than surrender, though, the Gauls became enraged. The Romans continued to besiege cities, and though with less successful results, their presence was being felt. More Gauls were switching their allegiance to Vercingetorix, and the odds were growing against Caesar. Rather than retreat home, though, the Romans consolidated all their forces and advanced north.

The advantage was to the Gauls, and with their ability to conduct themselves as a mobile force with a strong cavalry, they had the ability to wage a war of attrition. Vercingetorix wanted to strike hard and fast, but Caesar had a similar thought as to tactics, and, with the help of his Germanic cavalry, he inflicted a quick sting on the Gauls.

While that defeat should have been viewed as little more than a temporary setback, the Gauls viewed it as devastating, and their warriors began a retreat to a hillside city called Alesia. Abandoning his strategy of quick strikes against the starving Romans, Vercingetorix took his army into the city, quickly threw up additional defenses, and then waited for the invader.

Caesar knew the numbers were against him, but he also knew that this event was a break-even gamble for him. He would accommodate the Gauls, and as his soldiers arrived at Alesia he saw opportunity when no one else would have. Alesia was on a steep hill, bounded by rivers on either side. A direct assault was bound to be fruitless, so Caesar took an innovative approach. He would turn Alesia from a safe haven into a trap. He immediately had his men dig a series of ditches around the hill, and adjacent to those ditches he built timbered walls and siege towers such as he had used at Avaricum.

When completed, the ditches and walls surrounding the base

of the hill would, incredibly, extend for 10 miles. The ditches to the front of the walls were reinforced with tree branches that would make it difficult for the Gauls, should they try to escape. The Romans dug other pitfalls to their front and littered the ground with stimuli—barbed iron spikes driven into the ground, which caused serious injury to any advancing troops. The practical effect was that any attempt to break out would stall when the pitfalls and ditches were reached, and at that moment the Romans would be close enough to reach the Gauls with slings, arrows, and fire. The works took about a month to build, and though the Gauls did attempt to stop the construction, it wasn't enough. They began to realize that they would be trapped inside Alesia and that their city walls had become prison walls. Vercingetorix had marched into the town with 80,000 men, and those would soon be competing with the inhabitants—women, children, and older men—who would also require food and water. The resources just weren't there. Such is the gamble when held captive in siege warfare, with a breakout or rescue as the only salvation.

The reality, though, was that Caesar realized his 50,000 men were also in danger. The Gauls might easily muster four times his number outside the walls, and he knew that the Gallic cavalry had escaped Alesia as his enclosing wall was being built. There was little doubt that they were riding for help. Caesar promptly sent men out to gather all the food they could find, while ordering others to build a fort for their own protection. But this couldn't be any ordinary fortress. By necessity it had to circle the entire wall he had just built around Alesia. So, facing outward, his men fell to completing a wall which must hold against the relief forces that the Gauls would send.

The Gauls did arrive, and with more than 200,000 men outside the walls, their numbers would surely wash across the Romans. The men outside could not communicate with those trapped inside, but Vercingetorix was somehow able to launch an assault from within as soon as he realized that his relief was attacking. The Gauls advanced on the walls at one of its weaker points, near the river, and felt certain that they could open a breach. The breakthrough happened as expected, and the Romans were called from their towers to seal the gap. It would be hand-to-hand fighting in the classic Roman style. The front lines were a shield wall, swords glistening, helmets and mail, centurions in a place of honor and certain death, and legionaries with a discipline that defied the odds against them.

As the battle pushed back and forth, Caesar made two important decisions. First, he sent his cavalry around behind the advancing Gauls, which would result in a pincer movement. Then, to be sure that the second arm of the pincer would hold, he threw himself and his last men into the breach. As Caesar rallied his troops, his horsemen slammed into the rear of the Gauls, forcing them into disorganization. This unexpected assault disrupted the Gauls to the point that many began fleeing the battlefield, giving the Romans the opportunity to begin a chase that was certain death for anyone within the reach of a Roman pike or sword. The Battle of Alesia was over.

While the army outside the walls scattered across Gaul, the people inside realized that starvation would defeat them, as the victorious Romans merely waited and watched. Women and children were sent outside the walls, down to the Romans, where they begged to be fed. Caesar refused, and the end was obvious.

Vercingetorix rode into the Roman works, surrendered himself to Caesar, and was taken to Rome as a prisoner. The war was over.

This is a tough battle for me because, I suppose, I'm usually rooting for the underdog. Vercingetorix had accomplished something amazing by uniting the Gallic tribes against a common foe, and he was extraordinary in convincing them to adopt his scorched earth policy. It was a good strategy in that an army the size of Caesar's could not survive long while being denied the basics of life. The Gauls had only to avoid a direct fight against the disciplined legions, and the result would likely be a demoralized army crossing back into Rome.

The Gallic chieftain might be forgiven for his quick retreat into Alesia, but not for his actions after it became obvious what the Romans were intending. At first, as the ditches were dug and the forests brought down for the walls, the Gauls made an effective use of their cavalry by repeated sorties against the builders. Against logic, though, Vercingetorix later sent his entire cavalry outside the walls to get help. That cavalry numbered about 15,000 men, and though it might be argued that those were mouths that no longer had to be fed, the more realistic argument is that the Gauls now found themselves trapped. They were left with no option for movement and no chance of improving their situation without outside assistance.

Inversely, Caesar realized the hazards of the status quo. He could no longer wander throughout Gaul looking for a fight, while allowing the Gauls to engage on their own terms. He needed a pitched battle, and he could not allow the situation to remain as it had been. His best option at success was to take action. Though his action was completely unconventional, he had faith in his abilities.

So many times in life we allow fear of minor setbacks to paralyze us, as Vercingetorix did at Alesia. But so often the best thing we can do is to confront our fears, face the battle before us, and immediately do something to effect a change for the better. It's as simple as saying, "I can do this," neglecting your irrational fear, and stepping forward to the challenge.

6

BE YOURSELF: THE BATTLE OF KORTRIJK

"It takes courage to grow up and become who you really are."
E.E. Cummings

My kids came home from school in their normal fashion: happy and hungry. As usual, they grabbed a snack from the pantry, got Snoopy ready for his walk, and headed out the door with me. It was a nice fall day and we all had a little spring in our steps. Our afternoon walk is, almost always, the best part of my day.

A few years ago, I got a bit of advice. When your kids get home from school, a great conversation starter is to ask what they did that was most fun that day. That turned out to be a great recommendation and usually helped us transition into other things like what they're studying, who their friends are, any problems with grades—anything really.

Cal offered an incredible and excited rendition of the games he had played at recess with his buddies, and how they were an assassin team that was "totally boss." Every kid had his own level of expertise, but there were no superpowers involved. At eight-years-old you apparently don't need superpowers any more. I was good with that, and loved his description of how his team saved the day with their extraordinary abilities at running, jumping, outsmarting, and so forth.

At 11, Ella was a little more restrained discussing her day, but had a couple questions about social studies and whether it would be OK if she went to the Bulldog Bonfire fundraiser. She'd pay for the ticket herself if I'd just say yes. Sure, not a problem.

Then, Cal quietly told me that he had something else he wanted to talk about. He was bothered about something and wanted me to listen. He said that there was an assignment that day at school and that he was supposed to write a goal that he had. For his answer, he told me, he had written, "My goal is to be me." The problem was then revealed: The counselor had collected his paper, handed it back, and told him to put down a "real goal."

But, Cal told me, to him that was a real goal. Then he poured out emotion as I'd never seen from him. He announced that Ella is awesome at dancing and I'm a good writer, but that he didn't think he's good at very much. He said he wanted to do a lot of things, but he wasn't sure that he's very smart, even though his grades were good. He liked playing at recess and enjoyed taekwondo, but he wasn't on any sports teams so he didn't know whether he'd be good at football or baseball. He thought he was popular, but wasn't sure how that helped with goals. He said he really wasn't sure about a lot of things, and that he didn't think it could be fair to have to make decisions like that when you're only eight. So we discussed that goals can be as simple as cleaning your room, going to college in 10 years, or buying a cattle farm when you're older.

By that time, we were back home, and I must admit that he was crying. Honestly, I was doing my best to hold back my own tears. Ella was as sweet as she could be, telling him that he was indeed "so good" at everything—that he should never have to worry about any of that.

As our conversation wound down I asked him what he ended up writing to make the counselor happy. He replied that he finally wrote that he wanted to be an army tank driver. That's a great goal, no doubt. Still, I think perhaps that Cal was on to something with his original answer. I'm not blaming the counselor for wanting a concrete answer—I totally get it—but I think his original reply held more merit and offered more thought and consideration than she realized. The best chance of success in this world comes when we are ourselves and when we recognize that we can't be, and shouldn't try to be, anyone else. I'm happy with his original answer: "My goal is to be me."

*****

The Battle of Kortrijk — 1302

"Be yourself. Everyone else is already taken."
Oscar Wilde

When it comes down to it, you're really the best judge as to what you can do and what you want to do. You should approach your life with that understanding. It's truly a strength to understand where you excel and to be able to maintain that as a focus. At the 2016 Olympics, following a defeat in a soccer match, the U.S. goalkeeper called her opponents "cowards" because they played the game that favored their style of play. Her words reflected the pain of defeat, but they also showed the limits of her understanding of the loss.

In contrast to that soccer game, the battlefields of history offer several examples of armies falling to defeat because they tried to fight in the manner of their opponents. But one of the most interesting battles in European history gave victory to the side that tried something innovative for the time: fighting with its own character in mind. In life you have to be yourself and go to your strengths. Do what you enjoy and play the game of life as you like. You'll be happier and more successful than you've ever imagined.

***

Pieter stood at the ready, as he had for quite some time, awaiting the attack. He was to the front of the lines, and though nothing more than part of a citizen militia, he felt a certain sense of security. To his left, and not so far away, was the River Leie, protecting against an advance from the north and curving so as to offer further protection from the rear. To his front was a small, muddy stream that could be forded, but which was an impediment to heavy horses. Beyond that, to strengthen their position, his army had also dug ditches and pits, many disguised or hidden, in the hope that they might also serve to slow the advance of the enemy. Around him were other men of Flanders and, though most were not soldiers, they had trained extensively and felt they would be able to stand firm against the invaders. Their weapon of choice was the goedendag: a long club with substantial weight, iron-spiked on its end, and used either as a spear or a heavy mallet which could smash into the skulls of the enemy. The front line consisted of pikemen who would be better equipped to stop any initial push against their massed wall of men. Fluttering across the scene were the flags of the guilds, and Pieter's simple uniform identified him as a weaver, an important and earned vocation. Here stood 9,000 men from all across Flanders, secure only in the knowledge that they had discipline and a camaraderie that must surely prevail this day. Across the brook from them, ready to put down this revolt of commoners, stood the finest that France had to offer. With more than 2,500 knights and 6,000 foot soldiers under the command of Count Robert of Artois, the French were ready to make quick work of this rabble of simple guildsmen. Robert's crossbowmen had begun the battle with a sting of arrows that forced back the advanced archers of the Flemings, and his infantry stepped forward and began to push against the assembled men of Flanders. Pieter knew that the knights were only waiting for their opportunity, but his focus now had to be surviving the professional infantry that was pressing him. To his rear he could hear his own army's bugles sounding the alarm, and his purest hope was that the reserves were coming his direction. He knew that foot soldiers had little chance against knights, especially fighting such as these, but he had to trust his training and his faith in himself, and to fight in his own method. He said a short prayer as the first of the French infantry crossed the brook, but stood his ground and slammed his goedendag into the helmet of the man approaching to his front. He was now a soldier.

It was July of 1302, and the Franco-Flemish War was in its fifth year. Politics and economics were tightly entwined in the County of Flanders. Even though large parts of Flanders were technically under French rule, many of the cities, such as Ghent and Ieper, had become rich in the cloth trades and were governed as though autonomous. In the past some cities had even aligned themselves with the English when that was to their benefit. The Flemish were good customers of English wool, and trade between the two areas was vital to the British and the Flemings. The Low Countries were experiencing incredible growth in trade and population, and the wealth and power centered around some of these cities had created a peculiar system that sometimes created a bit of rivalry between the counts, the burghers, and the guildsmen. While the title of count was one of royalty, the burghers were city officials who often held the real power in the cities. But lately that power was often challenged by the guildsmen. The guilds were associations of tradesmen: weavers, drapers, carpenters, merchants, and so forth. Not only did these guilds create many of the goods, they also policed their own and set and maintained price structures. Beyond that, as prominent citizens, they formed themselves into military units to protect their cities from attack. As one might imagine, these groups and people often had difficulty working together, and there were stresses. While a particular policy might benefit one group, that same policy might severely harm the other.

In normal times these stresses played out with smaller military maneuvers, sometimes city versus city, sometimes purely homegrown treachery. But these were not ordinary times. The

French king, Philip the Fair, had designs on much of what we know today as France, and he had a particular interest in the County of Flanders. In response, the Flemish had made an agreement with King Edward I, or "Longshanks," of England. While Edward had an interest in trading with the Flemish, his primary motivation was retaining control of Gascony, which Philip the Fair was claiming.

These were not normal times for the English, either. King Edward was dealing with something even bigger back home: a war with Scotland. William Wallace and his Scotsmen were playing havoc with the English, so Edward accepted a compromise with the French and sailed back home to deal with Wallace, leaving the Flemish to their own protections.

Philip the Fair was reaching the limits of his endurance with many in the County of Flanders. He had imprisoned their leader, Count Guy of Dampierre, as well as the count's oldest son, and had expected that to be that. In Flanders, though, there were still schisms. While most Flemish cities were advocating independence from France, their own nobility was growing wary of the power and influence that the commoners and guilds were gaining, so the majority of nobles aligned with the French.

The town of Bruges had maintained a virtual monopoly in the woolen trade with England, and that monopoly had made its traders rich. So, when King Edward of England began dealing directly with the customers for his wool, the traders were angered at their loss of revenue. They appealed to the French king, who promptly stationed French troops there to enforce the monopoly. That action infuriated the Flemish in Bruges, and, led by Pieter de Coninck and Jan Breydel, they staged an uprising against the French garrison. In the quiet of a May night, the Flemish rose and went from house to house, requiring the men suspected of being French to pronounce the phrase "schild en vriend." A simple Flemish shibboleth meaning "shield and friend," it was a difficult thing to pronounce for native French speakers. Anyone unable to speak the proper pronunciation was immediately killed. Two thousand French soldiers perished that night.

The massacre emboldened the Flemish, and the militia led by de Coninck and the grandsons of the imprisoned count began to expel the French. This general uprising infuriated King Philip and he responded by assembling knights and troops from France and beyond to quell the rebellion. Kortrijk had remained in French hands, through the rebellion, and its castle was being besieged by the Flemish. Because of that, it became the natural destination for the French marching north. The French army was led by Count Robert of Artois, an experienced soldier, and one who had previously defeated the Flemish in battle. He could imagine no circumstance in which he could lose a battle to such rabble, and he allowed his troops to devastate the Flemish countryside as they advanced toward Kortrijk.

For their part, the Flemish quickly learned of the French advance and called upon men from all of Flanders and the Low Countries. These troops were primarily men of the various guilds, other militia, and some farmers. There were only about 10 knights on the Flemish side and few professional soldiers of any type, so they could only rely on their practiced discipline and tactics. They also had two other advantages: geography and time. Kortrijk is situated on a river, and that, combined with a larger brook, gave them the opportunity to divert water into the area east of the town. The river was a natural protection to the rear and the left, so they created ditches and hidden traps where the French must advance. While these ditches would serve as barriers to infantry and cavalry, the resulting marsh would specifically be a hazard for the knights riding their chargers. Keeping the castle surrounded so that the French garrison could not escape, they made use of every minute for battlefield preparation. Meanwhile, their opponent approached from France.

And what an opponent it was. At the front, 2,500 armored knights led the advance, with a complement of 1,000 crossbowmen, 1,000 pikemen, and various other soldiers—bringing the number up to around 8,500. The French had an added advantage in that they had been informed of the traps that the Flemish had laid. In fact, they had purchased a map showing most of their locations, including the flooded ditches. The banners of the nobility flew in the July breeze while the horses, complete in their trappings, snorted and pawed in anticipation of battle.

On the Flemish side stood about 9,000 men, numerically similar to the French. They understood what was about to happen, and they were ready. Organized by guild, they stood assembled and waiting for the assault. Pikemen were in the front as the best hope to stop the crash of cavalry into the ranks, and in the second line stood the men with their goedendags. Most importantly, they stood with discipline, recognizing that they were not professional soldiers. But if they could be who they were—well-trained militia—they might have a chance. Could they be the first infantry to successfully hold back a charge from mounted knights? They had to be. Their leaders instructed that they would not be allowed to take booty or prisoners, under penalty of death, because any such distractions would surely be fatal. They said their prayers and made their confessions to the priests, then stood their ground.

The French opened the engagement in classic style with a flurry of arrows from their crossbows, and the Flemish replied with their own. But the Flemings were at a distinct disadvantage in this type of warfare, and when their arrows were all spent, they cut their bowstrings and threw their crossbows to the ground, hoping to slow the advance of the French horse. They then fell backward to a better gap of distance. With the softening of their lines, they knew that the French infantry would soon be moving forward.

The French foot soldiers began their advance, and there was the expected push and shove of battle. The knights were concerned, however, that they would not gain their expected glory, so the infantry was recalled from the line of battle and ordered to return to the rear. This action would give the cavalry the ability to take their place and earn the honors of the victory. But as the knights charged into the melee, they were slowed by the ditches and marshes, and their lack of speed made them vulnerable to the Flemish. Any knight who found himself slowed as he approached the first two rows of Flemings was soon dragged from his horse, usually suffering the full force of a goedendag smashing into his armor. Along the line there were breaks in the defense, but they were soon sealed. Only once was there a real threat, but that was mitigated by a Flemish knight who had remained loyal. He rapidly recognized the problem, and came forward with his men and sealed the gap. The French in the castle saw the disaster that was happening, but their attempted breakout was stopped by the men of Ieper, who were guarding the castle doors.

Robert of Artois decided to send another wave, which he would lead himself. He would not be beaten by townspeople, and if he could cause a quick breach in the lines, that should be enough to carry the day. He galloped forward on his war horse, Morel, which carried him into the first lines of the Flemish. Robert actually succeeded in breaching the lines and even secured a piece of a large Flemish banner. But, as with the knights before him, he was surrounded and pulled from his horse. He screamed and begged for the life of his prized warhorse, not realizing that the rules of chivalry had been suspended for this battle. In fact, as his horse was slaughtered, he heard the Flemings protest that they did not understand French. Only then did he realize that he was not going to be captured and ransomed. The last sound he heard on this earth was the strike of a goedendag as it crashed into his helmet.

Witnessing the rout occurring in their front, the French infantry began to run. The footmen were soon overtaken, while any wounded on the field were permanently dispatched. Some of the Flemish knights who fought with the French begged for mercy in their native language, but the militia was under orders to kill anyone wearing spurs. It was a slaughter as never before seen in European history. The pursuit of the French lasted five miles. The ultimate humiliation was delivered to many of the knights as they succumbed to the final blows of carpenters and weavers.

When the battle was over and the day had passed, more than 1,000 knights and nobles had been killed. Five hundred pairs of golden spurs—worn only by knights—had been taken from the battlefield and given to the local church for display. To this day, the Battle of Kortrijk (also known as Courtrai) is more often called the Battle of the Golden Spurs. For the first time in history, men on foot had withstood a charge by knights, and they had done so by remaining true to themselves and their abilities. Simply, they stood as they were: disciplined and trained men fighting to the best of their ability and working to their strengths.

This battle is really a story of success, when success was unlikely. The concept of militia standing against knights and cavalry was one that was unproven, but the Flemish guilds had trained as if they were a brotherhood, and they stood as such that day. The militia of the early 14th century was trained primarily to react to and defend against their own Flemish cities. The men of the guilds had trained, but even they realized that they would likely never be able to fight as professional soldiers.

An amazing fact regarding this part of history is how the commoners (for lack of a better word) reacted to the threat. In just a few years they had felt abandoned by their count, the king of France, and the king of England. They had only themselves to rely upon and had to stand in the only way they could: shoulder to shoulder, pikes in the front, goedendags nearby, and all without a glimpse of chivalry. It would be war, and they would fight in their own form and in their own fashion.

Count Robert of Artois should probably be forgiven for his rash charge in this battle. Commoners had never held against knights, and, from his perspective, there was little reason to believe that this time would be any different. Yet a good understanding of the guilds would imply that the common man in the Flemish lines might have felt differently. They knew their limitations, yet they marched to Kortrijk from towns all around Flanders—even from Ghent, which had declared itself neutral. Importantly, they fed from a madness of the nobility that had always governed them. Robert of Artois fully expected mercy as he was taken from his stallion, but he was vain and ignorant, not realizing the pain and fear that he had caused these people.

In retrospect, there was only one way that the Flemings could defeat the French and that was in their own method. Armed with the simple weapons they had trained with, and fighting with the methods that best suited their strengths, they took their only real option. They were not knights, but they could fight as brothers—not for glory, but for shared victory. Of all the ancient battles, the lesson here is arguably the best. Be yourself and be true to who you are.

7

SOME BATTLES MUST BE FOUGHT: THE BATTLE OF THE ALAMO

"Courage is fear holding on a minute longer."
General George S. Patton

Amy was one of the coolest chicks ever, a college friend. She was a sorority girl (Phi Mu, she'd have me tell you), but never let herself be defined that way. Smart, but possessing a coolness that made her seem casual under all circumstances. She brightened every party she ever attended and was always handy with a mix tape or two. With Amy you never knew whether the next song would be beach shag music, something New Wave, or maybe a little Springsteen. I liked that about her, and so did everyone else.

I lived in the Sigma Chi house in Knoxville, and Amy loved to drop by and hang out with me and my roommate. Like one of the guys, she always called us by our last names. "Turner, where's Sanders?" That cool factor, you know. We rode around in her Chevy convertible and blasted out whatever she was in the mood for, hit the dive bars, and danced at concerts by Jimmy Buffett and The B-52s.

But, beyond cool, Amy was curious, smart, and motivated. I remember her coming to my parents' house one weekend because she wanted to learn more about farming. She once invited me to speak to her book club because she said as a Memphis girl she should know more about the Civil War. It was that sort of thing that always struck me as so nice about Amy. She could talk on almost any topic, and I enjoyed that immensely. But she also had fun and always knew the place with the best cover band and half-price appetizers.

But life goes on. I moved to Nashville and we lost touch, even though I was pretty sure she had moved there, too. Purely by accident, I ran across her at a restaurant one night. We both had been stood up by friends, so had a chance to catch up. She had gone to work with an insurance company, but thought there was more she wanted to do in the world. She told me that she was considering going to law school, which was obviously a good choice for someone like her. After a few months we lost touch again, simple to do in those days without cell phones and Internet, when phone numbers often changed with addresses.

I found her again, as expected. What I didn't expect was how. One afternoon she pulled into my driveway and let me know that she had bought a house a few months earlier and that it was just down the street. She apologized, but had enrolled in law school and that was taking a lot of her time, and of course there was always something else going on. She felt bad, but should not have. Law school was a challenge and a battle, and no doubt she was going to succeed. She'd also met a guy there, and I was glad about that, too. She deserved all the good stuff in the world.

Eventually she married that great guy, and I was married a few months later. Almost like a joke, she had a daughter and I had a daughter. She had a son and I had a son. Sometimes I'd see her pushing a carriage and sometimes she'd be jogging, but we'd always stop to talk, and she was unfailingly the same old Amy.

Then there was an odd day. We stood there talking and she mentioned that something had been bothering her legs. She wasn't sure what it was. I joked about us getting older, and she said she wasn't ready. Then, for several weeks, I didn't see Amy. There were a lot of different walking routes in our neighborhood and I thought I was just missing her. I discovered that she had become more concerned about what was happening to herself and had gone to see a doctor. The diagnosis was devastating: ALS, also known as Lou Gehrig's Disease.

Lou Gehrig's Disease has no cure and is usually fatal in just a few years. Doctors really don't know what causes it. For some people it may be genetic; it's possible that some external factors come into play. For others it's just random. I didn't know any of that when she told me. All I knew was that the coolest chick I had ever known, always vibrant and smiling, was dying. I couldn't believe it. (I still can't, to be honest.)

Still, Amy was a fighter, and I knew she wasn't going to let this beat her. She couldn't be defeated, as far as I was concerned. She began blogging and had hundreds of cheerleaders out there. She let us know what she was dealing with every step of the way and the lengths she was going to in her brave attempt to stop or slow the disease. Her priority was her husband and kids, and they traveled, had fun, always loved, and did everything they could to keep life in its proper perspective. She even kept up her work as an attorney as long as she possibly could. She loved the Lou Gehrig quote about considering himself the luckiest man on earth and used it on her blog. To the other side of her reality, though, she was willing to go anywhere and try anything to extend her survival. She once told me that even if something failed, it made it more likely that the next person could move on and try something else. I admired her for realizing that she might not save herself, but there was going to be someone else after her who could benefit from everything she tried.

Amy actively recruited walking teams to help raise money for an ALS cure. She did more good than even she might have imagined. I think "Amy's Army" eventually raised more than $100,000 for ALS research. I would read her blog and think she was going to beat the odds. She'd email sometimes, usually with updates about friends we held in common. Things felt normal, and I began to think she might be one of those who could beat the odds for many years—a Stephen Hawking. Then came an email that was different than the rest. She was asking me and a couple other Sigma Chi brothers to remind her of some of the songs we had on our fraternity mix tapes. I can't recall exactly what she said, but I knew that she was picturing the end. She had given all she had, and the fight was done.

Just a few weeks before her passing, when she no longer had her voice and struggled with the loss of her normal eloquence, she wrote a few simple lines in a blog post. I can hear her saying, "Turner, that's terrible grammar and you shouldn't quote me."

But I have to, because regardless of grammar it's a perfect statement that I want the world to hear. From my friend Amy, in the unfiltered voice that made me and so many others love her: "Get off your ass, and stop being stressed along with smoking, overeating, or sad or whatever your vice. Do something for yourself and walk a mile. I would kill to be able to do so. Not being preachy."

Amy's funeral was the largest that I've ever attended and will likely stay that way. Hundreds of friends were there, following her wish that people wear color rather than black. I wore Tennessee Volunteers orange and pictured her dancing with me as we sang "Margaritaville" together. I believe that the colors she wanted at her funeral signified that she never surrendered, and that she would never want any of us to give up. She would not accept defeat. Her lesson was simple: Some battles are worth fighting.

*****

The Battle of the Alamo — 1836

"The harder the conflict, the more glorious the triumph."
Thomas Paine

History is replete with stories of last stands. Most failed, a few succeeded, and several could be debated as to what was truly the end result. A few of these quickly come to mind.

The story of the three hundred Spartans (with a thousand friends) defending the pass at Thermopylae against tens of thousands of Persians is probably the most famous of the ancient battles. Betrayed and annihilated, they are still remembered as heroes defending their homes.

The Crimean War gave us the charge of the Light Brigade, when English cavalry mistakenly charged into a valley of Russian heavy artillery. They did not stop until reaching the guns, and their casualty rate stands as evidence of that. I suppose it's correct to say that the Russians lost that war, but there's a good argument to be had that the peace treaty brought no real resolution.

The Battle of the Little Bighorn brought the destruction of Lt. Colonel George A. Custer and his men while fighting Lakota and Cheyenne warriors. Sometimes called Custer's Last Stand, it's more a testament to what happens when a commander combines bluster, blunder, and ignorance.

World War II brought the Battle of Bastogne, infamous because of the reply given to the Germans when they asked for the Americans to surrender: "Nuts." The Americans were able to fight and hang on until they were rescued by elements of Patton's Third Army.

I look at these battles, with their differing results and meanings, and try to learn from them. It's an old expression of thought, but it is important to choose your battles. Many are obviously worth it, some never are, and others you won't know until much later. Regardless of outcome, the only battles that never really matter are those that are forgotten.

***

Sleep had been almost impossible for the last few days. The incessant cannonade had kept the entire fort on edge for almost two weeks, and the men all welcomed the quiet that had come in the last few hours. But that silence was suddenly broken by bugles and shouts from just outside the walls. William realized that the attack was happening, leapt from his cot, and climbed to the top of the parapet. In the early dawn it was impossible to see very well, but the sounds were enough to let him know this was the major assault they had been dreading. As commander of the fort, he had ordered sentries placed outside to warn of a surreptitious assault, but they had apparently been surprised and killed. His men were beginning to rush to defend the walls, but the scaling ladders were already being brought forward, and the Mexican troops were scrambling to the top. Jim Bowie was sick and unable to fight, but David Crockett and the Tennesseans were certainly going to do their part. The reality, for William, was that he didn't have the luxury of directing his men and hoping they would stick to the rehearsed plan. At this moment he was commander and soldier, and his task was to fight. He grabbed a shotgun and surveyed the scene. Hundreds of Mexicans crowded outside, awaiting the opportunity to cross the walls. William would never see them enter the fort, because in the first moments of the onslaught a bullet struck him in the forehead. The body of Colonel William Barrett Travis crumpled onto the parapet. His letters for help had been neglected, his men were outnumbered ten to one, and the revolution was dying with them. There would be no help for the men of the Alamo.

It was March 1836, and there was discontent and rebellion in Mexico. Texas, in particular, seemed to hold most of the zealots. Mexico had successfully gained its independence from Spain just fifteen years earlier and had been seen by many as a land of opportunity. Following a brief flirtation with a monarchy, the reorganized structure of government was not that different from the adjoining United States. Land was cheap for those willing to follow Texas law, and Mexico was willing to accept immigrants who would follow its laws and traditions. Many Americans saw this as an opportunity, and they arrived in droves.

In many ways the politics of Mexico reflected those of the United States. After their break with Spain and the removal of a monarch, the Mexican population was eager for self-rule. Many desired a republican form of government with a weak central government and a stronger focus on the states and territories. Americans were contributing to that way of thinking, and many were known to carry copies of the United States Constitution on their person as if they were still in the U.S. Opportunity abounded.

Then came Santa Anna, formerly a royalist, but a man who eventually supported the separation from Spain. Santa Anna quickly rose in status and found himself as president—though disinterested—of the United Mexican States. Almost certainly a narcissist, Santa Anna began to call himself the "Napoleon of the West" and set himself up as a dictator. He suspended the Mexican Constitution of 1824, dissolved the Congress, and convinced the military to back him. Unrest swept across the nation, but Texas, without a doubt, would be a problem.

Texians (the residents of Texas) were a little of everything: Mexicans, Indians, Spaniards, and a grand assortment of anyone arriving from the United States. The Mexican Constitution of 1824 was not based on the U.S. Constitution, but it was similar and relevant to the Texians—natives and settlers alike. The reality at the time was that many Texians weren't looking to establish a separate government. They simply wanted adherence to the Constitution, which would rid themselves of a dictator (Santa

Anna) and deliver back local control. Still, it is true that other settlers began to believe that Texas would function better as an independent state, separate from Mexico. While those two political ideals bounced back and forth in Texas, we know that dictators rarely relinquish power. Santa Anna certainly would not be an exception.

It became obvious that the Texians were willing to fight, so Santa Anna began marching soldiers toward Texas. Chilling, for those who were not native, was a directive from the dictator that all armed foreigners fighting against the government would be executed as pirates upon their capture. This was an obvious message to any Americans who might be convinced to join the Texas revolution. Likewise, U.S. President Andrew Jackson was officially holding to a political reality that Texas was part of Mexico, a sovereign country. He wanted Texas, but preferred to buy it.

Santa Anna was dealing with rebellion throughout the country, so he sent General Martin Perfecto de Cos to put a stop to things in Texas. The Battle of Gonzales, in October 1835, started the Texas Revolution, and General Cos was sent with a force large enough to immediately quell it. But, with a twist that we so often see in military history, a series of events forced General Cos to retreat. He withdrew his men to San Antonio de Béxar, and there they started to reinforce the city. They also began to restore the Alamo, an old Spanish mission that had previously been used as a fortress of sorts. Texians under Stephen F. Austin besieged the city, forcing the Mexicans to eventually consolidate their forces at the Alamo. The Mexican army was depleted through death and desertion, and, after a few days of fighting, General Cos was forced to surrender. The Siege of Béxar (San Antonio) was a huge success, and the rebels captured the city along with several Mexican cannons and muskets.

San Antonio was of strategic importance because of its location, and the Texians were determined to hold it. Using practically the same concept as the defeated Mexican army, they added a few personal touches such as parapets or catwalks around the interior of the Alamo and dug trenches inside the mission walls in the event that they were forced to fight from within the interior buildings. But while the Alamo had served as a fort for decades, it simply wasn't viable against modern weapons and siege tactics. How could a motley crew of rebels expect to hold it against a large army such as the one that would return with General Santa Anna?

Sam Houston was the commander of Texian forces. He realized that the small garrison occupying the Alamo was not capable of the type of defense required to hold it. He sent orders with Jim Bowie (the man with the big knife and an even bigger reputation) to have the cannons and arms removed, and to have the men evacuated. Bowie had married into a prosperous, local family and was familiar with the geography. He also knew several of the prominent men and families in San Antonio and understood the danger of the situation. Then something changed him. The more that Bowie talked with the commander and the men holding the fort, the more he felt their sense of patriotism, the distinct conviction that the Alamo must be held. While men were gathering 150 miles away to discuss a Texas declaration of independence, the ardor of the men who were willing to stand and fight here was remarkable. Perhaps it was a foolhardy decision, but he understood the importance of this location—of this time and place. With a firm resolve and reinforcements, the Alamo just might be held. Bowie disregarded his orders and vowed to stay and fight.

Estimates vary, but there were likely fewer than 250 men (and a few female family members) in the Alamo in February of 1836. Of these, the most famous was easily David Crockett. Crockett, a Tennessean, was not only recognizable but also immensely popular. His tall tales were the stuff of books and plays, and he was a master at self-promotion. Americans knew Crockett as a raconteur who could fight a bear with just his hands, grin a raccoon out of a tree, or hit any target with Old Betsy (his Pennsylvania rifle). Tennesseans knew Crockett as a congressman, one who was absolutely his own man when being a Jacksonian would surely have served him better. In fact, Crockett's bid for another congressional term had fallen short when he was beaten by a Jacksonian, and he decided to leave the state. Clad in buckskin and his trademark coonskin cap, he left from Memphis with a message to those who didn't vote for him: "You may all go to hell, and I will go to Texas."

Santa Anna found his travels north slower than expected due to poor weather, wet and cold, but was able to meet up with General Cos as he retreated south. If the traitors were still in San Antonio de Béxar, as he believed, his larger army would quickly defeat their handful of volunteers. His soldiers were armed with Brown Bess muskets and were well-dressed. While Mexican uniforms had a bit of variety, they were of a professional standard that would rival the best that Europe had to offer. Picture a blue, double-breasted coat with red lapels, white pants, and a tall shako hat complete with plume or pom. While a large number of Santa Anna's army was not quite as professional as their appearance, he would have them prepared enough to make war on the rabble he expected to meet at San Antonio.

It was certainly an interesting group awaiting the arrival of the Mexicans. While Jim Bowie (a colonel because of previous service with the Texas Rangers) commanded the volunteers, Colonel William Travis was in charge of the regular soldiers. The scenario wasn't perfect—a normal chain of command would have been better—but it was the best they could do under the circumstances. All the while, David Crockett (a colonel from his previous service in the Tennessee militia) kept the men entertained with his outrageous stories and fiddle playing.

Colonel Travis, of all the men at the Alamo, was most able to put a voice to the cry for liberty and independence. An attorney who had come west from Alabama, Travis penned letters that, while technically exhortations for reinforcements and relief, may be some of the finest cries for liberty ever written. All these years later, one can easily imagine him sitting behind the barricades composing the script that would still be relevant today: "Victory or death" and "never surrender or retreat." Still in his mid-twenties, Travis had been an early convert to the cause of Texas independence, and he would die for it. One of the last letters carried through the siege lines made clear that Travis would surrender if he thought he were fighting for anything less than complete autonomy for Texas.

The story of the Alamo is really one of frustration for its defenders. The Mexican army eventually made its way to San Antonio, surrounded the city, set up cannons, and raised the Mexican tricolor of green, white, and red. They also raised red flags to inform the Texians they would be offered no chance to surrender—there would be no quarter. Courier after courier was able to gallop through the Mexican lines with missives requesting help, but for the most part they were disregarded. A small group from Gonzales, perhaps thirty men, came to help—scarcely the relief that Travis needed and expected.

For thirteen days the Mexican army bombarded the Alamo, hoping to breach the walls and intending to drive the inhabitants mad. And for those thirteen days Travis resisted surrender, ordering his cannons to fire three times a day to let potential reinforcements know that he still held firm, that there was still a chance. Yet no one came. The few men of the New Orleans Greys stood uniformed and disciplined, their flag (soon captured by Santa Anna) outlined against the sky. The bulk of men, though, wore civilian clothing and hats, some in frontier buckskin. Bowie was sick in bed with typhoid, likely to die, regardless of the Mexicans. Crockett, almost 50, showed off his sharpshooting skills, and Travis wrote and planned and wondered whether he would ever wear the uniform he had recently commissioned. He then gave his men the chance to leave, with death almost certain. A few took him up on the offer, especially Tejanos with family in the area, but most remained. It was only a matter of time at that point.

At 5:00 AM on the morning of March 6th, the Texians were awakened by bugles calling "El Degüello." The song's dark, haunting notes signified that the Mexicans were assaulting with no intention of allowing survivors. In the darkness, Santa Anna had sent forward men to quietly assassinate the sentries posted outside the walls. He then ordered a general advance of men with scaling ladders. Those men assaulted the walls—north, south, east, and west—while lancers and cavalry patrolled the perimeter to make sure that no one inside could escape. No quarter.

I need to make a point about the irony of the Battle of the Alamo. While the men inside had sworn to fight to the end, history tells us that men will face reality and concede defeat when surrender offers them the only logical chance of survival. General Santa Anna wanted to be sure they never got that chance. He could have continued with the siege and eventually bombarded and starved those men into submission. But his strategy was one in which he would devastate and annihilate those men, convincing their fellow rebels that resistance was futile. The concept, from a battlefield perspective, was valid. But Santa Anna carried it too far.

The battle began with a rush to all four walls by the Mexicans and a destructive reply from the cannons inside. Mexicans fell by the hundreds as they attempted to breach the thick walls. Even though the cannon fire was devastating to the Mexicans, their numerical superiority gave them a monumental advantage, and they were eventually able to scale the walls. Once inside, their troops were able to fling forward the doors, and the way was clear for a wholesale slaughter. While individual Texians were able to fall back to houses, barracks, or the chapel, they were only buying a few last minutes of life.

The battle took just 90 minutes, and while we'll never know exactly what happened, we know enough. Travis was killed in the first moments of fighting, while Bowie was killed in bed, possibly shooting with a brace of pistols or slashing with his eponymous knife. Several groups of men made it outside the walls but were run down by Mexican lancers. Crockett was likely overwhelmed and captured at the end of the fighting. While we may never know with certainty about Crockett, we do know that some men were captured and killed after the battle had ended. This action upset some of the Mexican military, as they held aloft certain standards of honor. Then, with the exception of one Texian (he had a brother in Santa Anna's army), all the bodies were stacked, fueled, and burned. The dictator had refused even a proper service or burial in his attempt to make other rebels cower.

The Alamo had fallen. Santa Anna released the women and Colonel Travis's servant, Joe, to go and tell what had happened. There was disbelief in Texas. Three weeks later came the Goliad Massacre, where the Mexican army captured and executed almost four hundred prisoners. The last man killed was their commander, Colonel James Fannin, who had made three last requests: that his personal possessions be sent to his family, that he be shot in the heart, and that he be given a Christian burial. Instead, the soldiers divided up his belongings, shot him in the face, and burned his body with the rest of the Texians killed that day. The events at Goliad were some of the most despicable in the history of warfare, to the point that many Mexican officers wanted no part in what were little more than executions.

The Battle of the Alamo and the Goliad Massacre did not have the effect that Santa Anna intended. While there were some who fled east for the safety of the United States, many men became hardened and vowed to remember their fallen comrades. They went forward with the chant, "Remember the Alamo. Remember Goliad." At the Alamo, Colonel Travis stood for a principle of liberty and a foundation of freedom. His letters to the outside world proclaimed that he and his men were chained to the ideal that they were at a time and place that mattered. So it was with him, Bowie, Crockett, and those known and unknown who perished in that old Spanish mission. Without their stand the revolution would likely have fizzled out as others in Mexico already had. Their fight, though lost, made the difference. Santa Anna was defeated and captured by enraged Texians just a few weeks later at the Battle of San Jacinto. Texas had its independence, and history will forever remember the Alamo.

8

BE KIND: THE BATTLE OF APPOMATTOX COURTHOUSE

———

"No act of kindness, no matter how small, is ever wasted."
Aesop

When my daughter was in elementary school, she loved attending "Doughnuts with Dads." That was a short, before-school event, typically lasting about 20 minutes or so. The PTO folks would bring in dozens of doughnuts, as well as milk and orange juice, and it was an opportunity for dads to have a chance to meet and talk with each other. The reality is that, even when strongly engaged in our children's education, parents rarely meet each other. I liked the concept, and Ella was counting on me going. It would make me a little late for work, but that was OK.

One of the important parts of the event, from the child's view, is a little note they write on construction paper that's taped to the wall. So, while you're having your first doughnut and juice, expect to be dragged over to the wall to find the work of art created just for you—probably embellished with hearts and an endearing message of "I love you, Daddy."

On this particular day I was in a little bit of a hurry, and Ella stopped by the gym to drop off her backpack. She said she'd be right back, so I went into the "Cub Den" with the thought of getting us in line for a quick breakfast snack. The lines were short, and I grabbed a doughnut and started talking to a father I'd met before. We chit-chatted for about five minutes, then I excused myself, hoping to find Ella in the middle of all the amped-up children running around. The room was big, but not that big, and I quickly realized that my daughter was not in there. Twenty minutes would go fast, and I knew she wanted to give me the art she'd made. Knowing myself, I probably uttered my typical, "Gee whiz."

I finished up doughnut number one and went down the hall searching for my "lost" daughter. I knew most of the teachers there, and one pointed me into the gymnasium. I walked in. There were a few children in there playing around, and in the far corner was Ella, sitting with a little girl that I didn't recognize. She looked up, I waved, in twenty seconds she had bounced over to me, and we were skipping down the hall to the party.

As is the nature of an event like that, it ended suddenly with a bell ringing, kids rushing to class, and dads hurrying to work. That afternoon I picked Ella up and asked her why she'd "ditched me" to hang out with the little girl in the gym. She told me that when she had gone to drop off her backpack, she had seen her classmate crying. She had gone over and asked if everything was OK, to which the little girl replied that she didn't have a dad and that she couldn't go to "Doughnuts with Dads." Ella, rather than just saying "sorry," sat there with her little friend, hugged her, and wouldn't let go. Only when I showed up and waved did she leave.

I'm still proud of what Ella did then, even though, today, she doesn't remember it at all. But the reality is that I remember all the little girls hugging each other at that event, and many others. I'll always picture Bella, Liberty, Anna, and those whose names I've forgotten, at the beginning of so many school days, hugging each other as if they would never be separated.

I don't suggest that Ella did something exceptional that day, even though my "proud dad" syndrome might vindicate the thought. In fact, I feel as if almost any other little girl would have done the same. I'm simply left questioning why they don't hug like that anymore, as they get older. Still, to me, her actions that day were something to admire. Ella saw a girl, much like herself, hurting as she might. And she sat with her and did her seven-year-old best to share the pain, which taught me a lesson.

The next year the "Doughnuts with Dads" organizers emphasized that anyone could attend the event, and I don't think that another child will ever feel left out again. In fact, I believe that little girl would have been gladly admitted to the party that year. It was just, I'm almost positive, a misunderstanding. But aren't so many things in this world?

Don't feel like you must have all the answers to everyone's problems. Sometimes you just need to be that hug or that shoulder to cry on. Be the guy who opens the door, the girl who smiles, the person who offers the smallest acknowledgment that we're all in it together. Because we are all in it together. Be the one who listens. Be the voice of those who can't—or won't—speak. Be kind.

*****

The Battle of Appomattox Courthouse — 1865

"Be kind, for everyone you meet is fighting a hard battle."
Reverend John Watson

There are worse things than defeat. It's a platitude, but one in which I firmly believe. Still, I can positively say that defeat can also be devastating. I wish it weren't true, but personal experience tells me that nothing stings more than being beaten. In war, in particular, defeat means many things—almost always terrible. Rarely does the history of warfare show us empathy or kindness. But it stands out when we see it, and I believe it deserves mention as a model of sorts. While the victor usually firmly places his boot on the throat of the vanquished, I have a prime example of how kindness matters.

***

The American Civil War was four years old in April of 1865, and it was obvious that the Southern Confederacy had been bled dry. General Johnston's Army of Tennessee was in North Carolina doing its best to stop Sherman's march, while General Kirby Smith was maintaining the status quo to the west of the Mississippi River. In Virginia, General Robert E. Lee had been stifled by overwhelming numbers at the Siege of Petersburg, and, ever the strategist, had decided to make a break for it with his Army of Northern Virginia.

General Lee informed President Jefferson Davis that Richmond must be abandoned, and while Davis and the Confederate government fled southward, Lee and his men would try to link up with General Johnston's army and fight as long as practicable. Lee's 30,000-man army was starving, and outnumbered at least four to one. Lee needed a good strategy and a lot of luck. Any breakout was contingent on Lee's men outracing the pursuing Union Army, and Lee still held to an optimism that he might find an opportunity to push through Sheridan's cavalry before Yankee infantry could engage. Still, as a pragmatist, he had written U.S. General Grant that he wished to discuss terms of peace—a discussion to which Grant agreed.

But there was one last chance, and Lee had to take it. Having retreated west to a small village called Appomattox Courthouse, Lee felt that he may have been able to move faster than the bulk of the Union infantry. He ordered General Gordon to attempt to open a gap through Sheridan's cavalry, large enough for a breakthrough and escape, but to inform him if he encountered any infantry. Infantry would be the sign that his Army of Northern Virginia was trapped, and that surrender would likely be his only option. Lee had watched the battle from a distance, and when Gordon called for reinforcements—yes, there was infantry to his front—Lee knew that the time had come. He had dressed that morning in his finest gray uniform, and, as he prepared to meet Grant at their appointed time, he outfitted himself as befitted a commander: felt hat, officer's sash, calfskin gauntlets, polished spurs, and a fine sword. Saying that he would rather die a thousand deaths than meet Grant, the reality was that his men had suffered enough, and he could no longer justify the fight.

Lee was humiliated to find himself in this position, but his hurt was just beginning. Instead of Grant awaiting him, Lee rode up to find a junior officer with a note from the Union commander. Grant would no longer be able to discuss anything other than total surrender, and simple terms of peace were no longer an option. Human nature being what it is, Lee may have briefly considered continuing the fight. But with the love and affection he had for his men, he wrote to General Grant that he would be willing to discuss the surrender of his army. Grant replied in the affirmative and asked Lee to choose a spot for their meeting.

It's almost impossible for me to overemphasize the fear and trepidation that Lee must have felt at that time. A student of history tends to look back at Appomattox Courthouse, knowing what happened, and think that the surrender unfolded the only way it possibly could have. That would be a mistake. The firebrands of the North were screaming for blood, and even though Lincoln had called for conciliatory measures throughout the war, there was every chance that even he might be overruled in some way. The reality is that Robert E. Lee and his Army of Northern Virginia had threatened the North for four years, that Lee was feared and hated, and that the first army to surrender might expect some of the harshest terms. History did not bode well for the Southerners that day, and I think that so much of today's reverence toward Lee is justified merely because he took the difficult option.

A private home was secured for the surrender. Victor and vanquished would sit at separate tables in the parlor. Lee arrived first, wearing, as previously mentioned, one of his finest uniforms. He looked ever the cavalier as he climbed the steps of the McLean home. Grant, who had to travel a distance to be there, arrived a few minutes later wearing a dusty, blue private's uniform. Even though the stars on his shoulders designated his rank, he stood in stark contrast with General Lee. There were a few pleasantries exchanged and a brief conversation leaning toward nostalgia, but for the most part this was an efficient meeting, with terms of surrender being written by Grant and offered to Lee.

As General Grant handed Lee his terms of surrender, Lee asked that his men be allowed to keep any privately-owned animals, so that they could return home and possibly make a spring planting by using those horses and mules. Grant immediately said yes. Lee also asked for tens of thousands of rations for his men, as they were starving. Grant was glad to feed his defeated foes, which was a show of kindness and a firm demonstration that the Union army had both overwhelming manpower and supplies.

As Lee left Appomattox Court House that afternoon, he knew that he had done the right thing for his men. Just that morning they had been fighting for their very lives, and that night they would be sleeping among the flags of truce, reciting the Soldier's Psalm, and eating their first decent meals since Petersburg.

As Grant rode away, he did so with a feeling of satisfaction, but he also felt the pain that was Lee's. As the news of surrender began to spread throughout the Union lines, there was exaltation. Men began firing cannons and rifles in celebration of their new victory—it was over for them. Yet Grant would not allow this type of demonstration to happen at the expense of the men on the other side. With as true an empathy as a victor ever held for his foe, he sent riders forward with word that those celebrations should cease immediately.

Grant ordered that there should be a formal surrender, but he also wanted it to be as simple an affair as possible. He scheduled the ceremony for three days after his initial meeting with Lee, and that's when we see a gesture that really made an impact. In fact, it may be the most incredible act that ever occurred during the surrender of an army.

After the terms of surrender had been written and agreed upon, Grant headed to meet with President Lincoln while Lee rode home to Richmond. The Confederate army would be surrendered by General John B. Gordon, while General Joshua Chamberlain had been chosen by Grant to accept the formal surrender.

Confederate General John B. Gordon was a native Georgian who had seen the fire of battle for four years, always leading from the front. An intrepid and aggressive commander, he was wounded many times during the war. While holding the Bloody Lane at Sharpsburg he was wounded four times before the fifth, a shot through the jaw, took him down. He fell forward with his face in his cap, and likely would have drowned in his own blood, had there not been a hole in the hat that allowed his blood to pour free. Gordon did recover, commanded a line at the Siege of Petersburg toward the end of the war, and was the man Lee tasked with leading the escape. On the morning of the day of surrender, it was Gordon who was leading the Confederate troops into battle, carrying forward into enemy entrenchments and capturing cannons. But it was also his duty later that morning, realizing that he could do no more without reinforcements, to let Lee know that he could go no further. He sent forward a colonel under a flag of truce, asking for a cease fire. The man that Gordon sent forward across the lines first met Union General Joshua Chamberlain and his staff.

Chamberlain was from Maine, the oldest of five children. As a youth, his father had pressured him to enlist as a military man, while his mother fervently wanted him to become a preacher. Emerging as his own man, he became a college professor (it's said that he could speak ten languages) at Bowdoin College in Maine. When the war erupted, he took a leave of absence and began his military career with an appointment as a Lieutenant Colonel. Like Gordon, Chamberlain led from the front. At the Battle of Gettysburg, he commanded the 20th Maine on Little Round Top, and with an uncanny anticipation of what was required on the Union left flank, he and his men held off the 15th Alabama as they attempted a crucial flanking maneuver. Chamberlain was slightly wounded at Gettysburg, and for his gallantry at such a crucial moment, he was later awarded the Medal of Honor. During the Siege of Petersburg he was severely wounded, and, in an effort to keep his men about task, he planted his sword into the ground as a crutch so that he could remain standing. He finally succumbed due to loss of blood, and his wound was thought mortal. In fact, he was given a battlefield promotion to Lieutenant General with the hope that it would take effect before he died. Somehow surviving, he rejoined the army, but was wounded again just a few days before the surrender. This final wound was also serious, being one that could have required the amputation of his arm.

Let me emphasize what was to take place at the formal surrender. After four years of intense fighting and sectional hatred, the Confederate army was being forced to march into the Union lines and give up their equipment, stack their arms, and deliver away their beloved battle flags. Bitterness was surely in the souls of men of both sides. That emotion would have been normal and not to be discounted. Generals Gordon and Chamberlain had both seen hard fighting, lost men, and nearly been killed themselves. Men follow by example, and the formality set aside for this surrender made it particularly difficult.

General Chamberlain brought in brigades familiar to him to accept the surrender. He placed them across the street, facing each other formally, as if in line of battle. Picture thousands of blue-clad soldiers at attention, eyes forward, with rifles at "order arms," meaning that the butts of the guns were resting on the ground. Formed up into regiments as if they were on the battlefield, over 25,000 Confederates began to march into the Union ranks to formally surrender. General Gordon rode at the head of the Confederate column, and as he reached the Union formation, Chamberlain noted that Gordon "was riding in advance of his troops, his chin drooped to his breast, downhearted and dejected in appearance almost beyond description." The pain and anguish of his former enemy brought forward an unexpected empathy, and Chamberlain immediately ordered his men to "carry arms." The order "carry arms" meant that the men quickly lifted their guns up, perpendicular to their shoulders. The action was a marching salute, which also created a loud smack as their hands changed position on their guns. No doubt the Confederates were startled by the sound, but General Gordon immediately recognized the order and action as one of respect. The Union army was honoring his men with a salute of arms! Gordon spurred and wheeled his horse toward Chamberlain, extended his sword and dropped it to his boot. He then turned to his own troops and ordered them to "carry arms." Honor answering honor, as Chamberlain later wrote.

Indeed, the formal surrender was a solemn affair, with a quietness from both sides that must have seemed surreal across that war-torn Virginia landscape. The bitterness of the past years was flowing away, and tears fell from both blue and gray. With the end of the ceremony, it was time to return to a new type of normalcy. Confederate arms were carried away for shipment to the rear, while individual soldiers tried to earn a few Yankee dollars by selling trinkets, tobacco, or their Confederate money as souvenirs. The next day most Southerners would be heading home, having promised to never take up arms again.

This isn't a fairytale story. There were certainly problems after the surrender, but the acts of respect and the terms given were an impetus for other Confederates to consider the same option. In particular, the Army of Tennessee surrendered a couple of weeks later, and with about four times as many men as Lee's Army of Northern Virginia. The mutual respect among the commanders, particularly between Gordon and Chamberlain, set a certain standard that carried on with the troops as they went their separate ways. Both men held the undying respect of their men, and after the war Gordon was elected governor of Georgia while Chamberlain was elected governor of Maine. Following his stint in politics, Chamberlain returned for a time to Bowdoin College, eventually becoming its president. He resigned that post when his old war wounds got the best of him.

I've always wondered why Chamberlain made such a conspicuous show of honor with that true act of kindness at Appomattox. If anything, one might think that he would have wanted to belittle his former enemies. You see, Chamberlain's wound at the Siege of Petersburg was very serious, having been shot through the hips and groin. From that day in 1864 when he could stand only by resting upon his sword, he suffered pain that lasted until the end of his life. He miraculously survived on the battlefield, but for the rest of the war, and including the surrender, he had to wear an early version of a catheter and a bag. He then endured several operations as doctors tried to correct the problem, without success. In fact, when he finally died in 1914, doctors diagnosed his death as having been caused by his wounds from 50 years earlier.

But there's something else you should know about General Chamberlain—something that I believe may be the key to his actions at Appomattox Courthouse. As a child he developed a stutter that was both embarrassing and isolating. He worked hard to suppress it, and with lots of diligent work with an able mentor, he was able to master the material required to gain admission as a student to Bowdoin College. While he was enrolled there, a professor of ancient languages showed him kindness, teaching him a method of "singing" through difficult words. The stutter was also likely a reason for his interest in mastering so many foreign languages. Still, the speech impediment stayed with him throughout his life and was always a consideration when he spoke, requiring him to hesitate and use pauses at moments when he knew he might stumble and stammer.

The fact is that General Joshua Chamberlain was in pain when he made the decision to salute the Confederate column at the formal surrender, and he also knew that he would be criticized for that action. He didn't hold on to the bitterness and anger that would have enveloped most men, and I think his lifelong experience of dealing with the humiliation of his stutter caused him to have an empathy toward the surrendering Confederate soldiers that others might not have possessed. He knew embarrassment and isolation, and he knew the redemption that a good soul might offer to a man who has nothing. We may speculate and guess as to reason, but there's no doubt that Chamberlain showed an uncommon compassion, decency, and kindness to his enemy. It's easy to be kind to friends, and even to strangers, truth be told. But to show compassion to an enemy, even though forgiven, requires a different standard. I admire Joshua Chamberlain for his actions at Appomattox Courthouse, and there is a lesson to be learned here. Whether you win or lose, be kind.

9

TRUST IS EARNED: THE BATTLE OF BOSWORTH FIELD

"The truest way to be deceived is to think oneself more knowing than others."
François de La Rochefoucauld

My employer, a medical group, was downsizing to get back to its core mission of providing the highest level of patient care. The accounting department, where I worked, was part of the administration being spun off to a management company. My job was almost certainly going to be eliminated in just a couple months, but at least I had time to search for a replacement.

I was a staff accountant on a small team of seven people: three staff accountants, one accounts payable clerk, one accounts receivable clerk, a payroll accountant, and an assistant who helped us with general accounting entry. We were a typical staff for a company that size, and we were all very good at our jobs. Our boss was the controller and had promised to help us in any way he could as we downsized. He assured us that he would be a great reference, would help us evaluate prospects, and wouldn't mind us leaving the office to do interviews.

The downsizing of our department fell into line with that of the entire company, and the layoffs began with assistants and others deemed less essential. As one might imagine, when the so-called "less essential" people were let go, the burden increased on the rest of us. I had been cross-trained at a previous job, so was adept at all aspects of accounting, especially payroll, which gave me an advantage. While I was actively searching for a new job, I knew that I would be one of the last to be let go in the accounting department. In fact, I hoped that I might be the last due to my payroll and tax experience.

Then came the perfect job opportunity. A friend who had been a co-worker at a previous job recommended an accounting position where she currently worked. Talk about luck! It was with the same management company that was taking over the administration of our medical group, and she told me that I was extremely qualified. My education was solid, my training from our prior employer was comprehensive, and the management company strongly desired someone with experience in the health care field. My friend would recommend me, and she felt that since we had similar backgrounds, this would be a dream job for me. It was the type of challenge I wanted. Beyond that, it came with a lot more money and as a promotion of sorts.

Dave was the staff accountant whom I had relied upon since

starting at the medical group. When he gave his two weeks' notice, that left just myself and the payroll clerk on staff. The payroll clerk had her eye on a couple of other opportunities, so I had the inside track on the opening at the management company. A couple weeks later I had an interview with them and felt so sure about my chances that I decided to quit sending out resumes. My boss assured me that he had sent a letter of reference. Everything looked good.

I kept waiting for the phone to ring, or perhaps even something in inter-company mail, as we were using that during the transition. But, nothing. I decided to ask my friend whether she had heard anything, and she promised to check. She finally got back to me a week later; the news was confidential and discouraging. She had gone to a confidant in their personnel office and discovered that my boss had not given me a recommendation. My supervisor, when asked for an opinion, had told my interviewer that I was not ready for that level of accounting. The real blow came when my friend told me the last bit of what she had learned. My boss had also asked for the position that I wanted so badly, and he had it. Some weeks later the payroll clerk found another job, and I was let go as one of the last administrative employees of the medical group. I had no job in waiting and no immediate options. I had made a terrible mistake.

The sort of betrayal that I experienced stung me, but I never told my boss that I knew what he had done. Looking back, there were obvious signs that he had not worked on my behalf. He never gave me a copy of the letter of recommendation, as he had with the others, and his visits over to the other company were obviously more than would have been required by a mid-level manager. I should have recognized that the job would be appealing to him, and that since he was also being let go, it would have been a great option for him. Mainly, though, I was upset at myself. I never considered that the job would not be mine, and when it fell through, I had no alternatives. Trust is required in our lives, but you should always consider whether the person you're trusting deserves it.

*****

The Battle of Bosworth Field — 1485

"The best way to find out if you can trust somebody is to trust them."
Ernest Hemingway

The battlefields of history are full of stories of treachery and duplicity, but one rises above all others. The Battle of Bosworth Field culminated in a betrayal that shook a kingdom, inspired a Shakespeare play, and set about one of the greatest mysteries of history. One more thing: It should never have happened.

***

The Battle of Bosworth Field was the last significant battle of the Wars of the Roses and was fought in central England in 1485. The Wars of the Roses were a series of battles between the Houses of York and Lancaster. While it's tempting to call it a civil war (and not at all incorrect), the war was more about which of these families would finally fight itself to the top of the British royal hierarchy. In fact, the Yorkists and Lancastrians were simply branches of the same Plantagenet family.

The latter part of the fifteenth century was an interesting time in Britain, to put it mildly. The Middle Ages were ending, and the kingdom had become an assembly of factions. Knights, men-at-arms, archers, and various and sundry hangers-on had been traveling to the continent for decades to participate in the Hundred Years War with France. English weapons, armor, and tactics had been refined and practically perfected during that war, though the British were finally forced to withdraw back to their island.

With all of these warriors returning to England, there came an opportunity for barons and earls to accumulate wealth and power. Britain suddenly found itself populated with experienced armies spread throughout the country to an extent likely never seen before, and absolutely never seen again. The reality is that a knight might owe a greater allegiance to the Earl of Oxford, as an example, than to the actual king.

By 1485, the Wars of the Roses had continued through three decades, complete with all the intrigue and treachery that would later find itself firmly entrenched in the stories of Shakespeare, Sir Walter Scott, and others. Richard III, of the House of York, had placed himself on the throne after the death of his brother, King Edward IV. By most accounts he had become an effective and fair king. Somewhat slight in build, with a modest curve of the spine, he was still a striking figure and a considerable soldier and man. His leadership on the battlefields of Barnet and Tewkesbury had cemented his reputation as a fighter. Richard had not actually been next in the line of succession but was petitioned to become king after his nephews were declared illegitimate. The two princes, who had been held in the Tower of London, soon disappeared, and King Richard III felt relatively secure after his coronation.

While it would take a book to describe the events leading up to this particular battle—and there are several I could recommend—suffice it to say that it was impossible to rise to become a king in 15th century England without someone wanting to take your place. In this instance, the usurper would be Henry Tudor, Earl of Richmond. Henry was prominent among the Lancastrians and had been biding his time on the continent, waiting for an opportunity to travel home and press his claims. Finally, he felt his time had come and sailed across the English Channel with a hired army.

When Henry landed in the western part of Britain, he began accumulating supporters, primarily from Wales and Cornwall, and then began marching toward London. King Richard III was fully informed but felt that this uprising would be quickly put down. It would certainly require a battle, but he was prepared—he was sufficient. While Henry and Richard were practically the same age, Richard recognized that his own military experience was far beyond anything that Henry had accumulated. The professional soldiers that had sailed with Henry were well schooled in tactics and methods, no doubt, but they were terribly outnumbered.

The reality was that homegrown opposition would likely be more a threat to Richard than this pretender from across the channel. Specifically, the Stanley family had long been a thorn in his side, and they had the ability to muster an army almost the size of his own.

As I previously mentioned, the various armies scattered about the kingdom had little more than a cursory obligation to the king, and the Stanley family had accumulated tremendous power and wealth. They were experts at promoting their family line and always seemed to find themselves gaining from English battles while never risking too much themselves. The Stanleys were simply devious, by any standard of the definition.

Henry Tudor had mustered about 5,000 men to meet King Richard III, though fewer than 1,000 of those were English. He was intelligent enough to realize his lack of experience and appointed John de Vere, the Earl of Oxford, as the commander of his army. The Earl of Oxford had significant battlefield experience, though he had never displayed military prowess. It would be a mistake to consider him a success story.

These are what might be deemed the classic days of English warfare. The last years of the medieval era, the knights wore full plate armor and their horses bore all the trappings. Both armies had archers and men-at-arms, and Richard's side had a good number of cannons, which it put to use as the battle began. Picture the classic image of a knight with armor glistening, surcoat displaying his coat of arms in brilliant colors, and the visor on his helm closed to stop the slew of arrows intended to blunt his rush forward. Flowing across the English summer sky was King Richard's massive banner, displaying his personal device of a white boar. The knights in Richard's company flaunted silver-gilt boar pins. On the other side of the field, Henry had chosen his native Welsh banner: a red dragon upon a background of green and white. The breeze lifted several flags and standards, making it simpler for men to remain as cohesive units on the battlefield.

Traditional tactics of the time called for opposing sides to set themselves into units known as battles, generally advancing as close-knit armed groups, then simply smashing into the opposing side. Often set as a vanguard with a battle on each wing, this method of assembly practically guaranteed a slugfest. The ground was gently rolling but damp and marshy in places, which could prove to be an advantage to a military tactician. The Earl of Oxford had concerns about his men and their numbers, so he declined at Bosworth to set his army into separate groups. King Richard did follow tradition and assembled his Yorkists into three fairly equal battles. Modern day discoveries of cannonballs mark Bosworth Field as probably the medieval battlefield with the most use of cannon, though there is no doubt that archers still played a considerable role. Cavalry as an organized force was only slightly used at Bosworth, possibly due to the marshy terrain of the battlefield as well as the practical aspects as to how the battle eventually unfolded.

The prelude to the Battle of Bosworth Field was typical, but with one huge exception never before seen to this extent on an English battlefield. There were four armies: King Richard's army of about 15,000 men, Henry's army of 5,000, and two independent groups belonging to the Stanley family, which totaled about 6,000.

Sir William Stanley and his elder brother Thomas, Earl of Derby, had brought their armies to the field, ostensibly as uncommitted to either side. The reality is that Richard knew the historical tendency of the Stanleys to choose sides just as a battle was decided, and he had taken himself a bit of insurance. He held George Stanley, son of Thomas, as hostage to serve as a guarantor of good behavior of the powerful Stanley family. King Richard left orders that George Stanley should be immediately killed if his father showed any sign of betrayal.

The battle began with conventional tactics for the times, with attempts to create and exploit gaps in the lines of the enemy. Of Richard's three battles, one was commanded by himself, one by the Duke of Norfolk, and the third by the Earl of Northumberland.

On the Lancastrian side, Henry's lack of battlefield experience was a liability, so he was sent toward the rear with his bodyguard. The Earl of Oxford would lead Henry's hired army, that being a hodgepodge of French, Welsh, Scots, and a very few Englishmen.

The Stanleys, 6,000 strong, simply watched and waited.

Both sides loosed arrows, which for the most part were ineffective at creating anything more than a little confusion in the lines. The plate armor of the times was very resistant to arrows, though a direct hit to an arm or leg might produce results. As mentioned before, Richard's army did include cannons, but they were apparently never able to create a gap in the lines.

The front became a confusion, and the swell of men pushed and swayed back and forth. Henry's vanguard was able to use the marsh as a slight bit of natural defense, enabling the Earl of Oxford to push his men forward and gain a headway into Richard's lines. Even though King Richard held numerical superiority over Henry, this was a critical part of the battle and he knew that he couldn't allow such a breach. The Duke of Norfolk, commanding Richard's vanguard, had been killed. This had an immediate effect on Richard, as he and Norfolk had been dear friends. But there was no time for grief because he needed to hold his collapsing center with a strong push back. Richard signaled to the Earl of Northumberland to come forward with his 7,000 men. In a hint as to the treachery on the battlefield that day, Northumberland stayed in place, leaving half of Richard's army completely out of the battle. I'll note that while it's certainly possible that the marshy, wet terrain played a part in Northumberland's choice to stay to the rear, Richard almost certainly saw it as an act of betrayal.

The king had to quickly evaluate what was happening. To his front he was being pushed back, and his reserve under Northumberland was still not advancing. The Stanleys remained at a distance, yet making no move at all to assist. He sent word to them for assistance, but received a vague response simply implying that they were on his side and just awaiting an opportunity to help. That response confirmed to Richard that these men were not his allies, and he ordered George Stanley be killed. In the confusion of battle, though, that was not done. The suspicion of treason had become reality, but he had to deal with the circumstances before him. Across the field, he saw the red dragon standard of Henry separate from the rest of the Lancastrian army and realized that Henry was probably riding to meet with the Stanleys. It was a risk that he wouldn't have considered just a couple of hours earlier, but he was no longer sure whom to trust, and he had to take matters into his own hands.

Richard quickly gathered a couple hundred of his most faithful knights and galloped to the spot on the field where Henry and his bodyguard were. The risk almost paid off. Richard came close enough to kill Henry's standard bearer, and was apparently within feet of personally striking a blow at Henry himself, who quickly dismounted and hid among his guards. Henry's Welsh bodyguard was able to hold off the Yorkists, though, and the fighting at this point was an extreme melee. Imagine the sounds of swords, halberds, and battle hammers striking metal, horses being pulled down, and the scream of men such as Richard's flag bearer, holding aloft the banner of the white boar even while his legs had been severed from his body.

Then came the Stanleys. In the final act of betrayal that Richard should have anticipated, they saw the chance to end the battle for the benefit of Henry Tudor, and they took that opportunity, pushing Richard and his men toward the marsh. Richard's horse became mired in the mud, and he was trapped. In the Shakespeare play *Richard III*, this is the scene in which he offers his kingdom for a horse. The reality is that Richard stood as a king and died as a king, and he went down swinging. Had he been offered a horse—and he may have been—he would not have accepted it. Several blows to the head killed Richard, dislodging his crown as he fell. Tradition holds that the king's golden crown was found in a hawthorn bush and that Lord Stanley immediately crowned Henry Tudor as Henry VII on Bosworth Field.

At Bosworth, Richard III was a victim of treachery and treason, and while most of us would have some empathy toward him because of that, there's a part of me that just wants to scream, "Could you not have seen that coming?" His best strategy would have been to have simply withdrawn his forces and then dealt with Henry Tudor and the Stanleys independently. At the very least, even after he had committed himself to battle, he should never have made such an impetuous charge across the field. The answer to my rhetorical question is, obviously, yes, he should have seen that coming.

Henry VII, after his coronation, made sure that men like the Stanleys would never have such power again, lest they someday become traitors to him. He outlawed such large, standing armies in Britain unless they served only the king. He realized that he could not trust anyone who might ever hold aspirations to his crown.

Trust is earned through a gradual process, but it can be lost or destroyed so quickly. You must trust people—you really must—but you also owe it to yourself to always consider your past experience with that person. Have they lied before, or have they always been true and the person you want and expect them to be? Are there "red flags" or something that just doesn't seem right? I'm not an expert at spotting liars and more than once I've trusted and been cheated. But I know that I've become better at knowing when someone seems self-serving, or when something just doesn't sound as I think it should.

Not to be lost in this conversation is the importance of being trustworthy, yourself. People will notice whether you're honest or truthful, and even one slip and they'll always have that in the back of their minds. Want a relevant example? Four years after the Battle of Bosworth, the Earl of Northumberland—who so famously did not bring his 7,000 men forward—was lynched by citizens of York who believed that he had betrayed Richard. Six years after that, Sir William Stanley once again attempted a bit of treason, this time against King Henry. Henry considered clemency, but knew the nature of the man, and needed to send a message about treachery. He had Sir Stanley beheaded.

There are people in this world who will lie and cheat, and that's on them. But your reputation is in your own hands, and that's on you. Trust because you have to, and be trustworthy because you owe that to everyone—especially yourself.

10

PRACTICE SELF-DISCIPLINE: THE BATTLE OF AGINCOURT

———

"The greatest remedy for anger is delay."
Thomas Paine

As my flight began its descent into Kansas City, the pilot came over the PA system to tell us that weather conditions were even worse than had been expected as we left Nashville. The prediction was now a minimum of eight inches of snow, with three to four inches already on the ground. Having grown up in Tennessee I had very little experience with snow like that, and as we dropped below the clouds my worst fears were realized. The ground was white—it seemed to be a blizzard—and I wasn't sure what to do. The Kansas City airport is quite a distance from downtown, where I was headed for an educational conference. I had a rental car waiting, but my experience driving in snow was limited to a country road with my dad's four-wheel drive pickup truck. I had been to Kansas City a couple of times before, but had only a basic knowledge of its layout and couldn't think of a way to get downtown without having problems on its bridges and hills.

My bags arrived quickly enough, and as I trudged through the snow to the shuttle stop I quickly ran through all my options: take a shuttle service, hire a cab to my hotel, or, as originally planned, grab my rental car. I decided that the original plan would be my best option, and, with any luck, I might be able to switch to a four-wheel drive SUV from my reserved mid-sized car. The driver of the shuttle told us that if we hurried along, we might be able to make it. In fact, he said, most businesses were closing, and that the roads were slick but not crowded. We had a chance, but there wasn't time to waste.

When I stepped off the shuttle bus, I had one mission: Get in and get out. I wanted a four-wheel drive, but if there were none available, take whatever and hit the road as quickly as possible. Inside the rental car office there was just one gentleman ahead of me. That was the good news. The bad news was that they were running short-staffed because of the weather. The customer in front of me identified himself to the lone clerk as one of their frequent renters, so I figured he would be quick and my turn would soon come. I was wrong.

The gentleman told the attendant that he had a reservation for a car with a GPS system to guide him, but that because of the snow he wanted to change that to a four-wheel drive SUV with a GPS. The clerk typed a few strokes on his terminal and told the man that he had just one four-wheel drive available, but it did not have a GPS system with it. The gentleman asked the logical question: Would it be possible to move the GPS system from the car to the SUV? The clerk replied that he could not switch the GPS system, but that he would be glad to change the man's car to the four-wheel drive.

It was then, almost in an instant, that the customer became belligerent. He began talking about how much business he brought the rental company every year and how important he was. With every word, the clerk furiously typed into his terminal looking for something else, hoping against hope that he could find an option. There were no alternatives. Take the car with the GPS, or take the four-wheel drive without one. The options were clear, but the customer would have none of it.

I turned away, caught in the embarrassment of the clerk, and saw nothing more than the snow continuing to fall. I couldn't believe this was happening. The most important man in the world was soon demanding to speak with the manager, and the clerk was more than happy to relinquish the argument. With a quick call to the back, the manager stepped in to assist and asked the clerk to move over and help me. It was the manager's turn to hear from the man, still furious, and his tirade seemed as if it would not end. He thought it impossible that he would not be accommodated. How could there be just one four-wheel drive left, and why could they not move the GPS?

The clerk stepped over to me, sheepish and ashamed at what I had seen. He quietly asked, as the rant continued twelve feet away, how he could help me. I told him that I had a reservation for a mid-sized car, but was worried about the snow and wondered whether there was an option for a four-wheel drive. He looked at his monitor, found my name, then smiled and looked up. He said,

"We have just one left, and it's yours if you say yes right now." I did, signed a paper, and was outside and leaving the parking lot—locked into four-wheel drive—in under five minutes.

I never understood the madness that overtook the gentleman that day and admit to rarely understanding when I see someone so enraged or so arrogant. There are absolutely times when we have justification for being angry and when we should be upset. But the inability to temper your emotions is a loss of control and an obstacle to anything positive that you're looking to accomplish. I've often wondered how things finally went for the gentleman that day, but my guess is not very well. If I could offer him any advice now, looking back, it would be this: Take a moment and breathe, lose the attitude, consider realistic options for the moment, and try to have a little understanding of the circumstances. Finally, never forget the age-old lesson: Choose your battles.

✶✶✶✶✶

The Battle of Agincourt — 1415

"If your opponent is of choleric temper, seek to irritate him.
Pretend to be weak, that he may grow arrogant."
Sun Tzu

Self-discipline is an interesting concept. Sometimes it requires an action and sometimes it's simply staying put and maintaining the status quo. Both can be equally difficult. To lose weight you may need to hit the gym (action), while also refusing dessert (status quo). Self-discipline also gets more complicated because your timing and temperament have to be right. Want a new job? Take action. Start networking, get your resume together, and start emailing. But also maintain the status quo. Keep working hard, do a good job, and never be the guy who makes everyone in the office uncomfortable while you moan and complain about every little thing. Self-discipline, in many cases, is simply knowing when it's best to stand up and when it's best to shut up. It's knowing how to choose your battles.

There's a difference between courage and discipline. History is riddled with stories of panic-stricken men who saved themselves by sticking together, remaining firm, and holding to every bit of self-discipline they could muster. I can also make a noteworthy list of battles where men were annihilated, when a bit of discipline might have saved them. One of the most famous battles in history was started by a group of men that took action, though the status quo would have suited them better, at least for just a few days more. Instead of success, though, they fell into a euphoria of greed, excitement, and anger, becoming statistics in one of the most lopsided battles of all time.

***

Henry ordered his men to advance toward the enemy, and they stepped onto the field with a slow but deliberate pace. That action smacked of insanity. They were severely outnumbered, they were starving and exhausted, and their army consisted mainly of archers. The field they were walking through was freshly plowed and muddy, requiring them to tread slowly. Further, their enemy had at least a couple thousand cavalry waiting for any exposure, so they had to keep in formation. But Henry had no choice. He was in enemy territory and his opponent's numbers were growing stronger every day. His best option was to play the antagonist, but the enemy knew that, and it was to their benefit to decline battle. Across the field were the finest knights in France with the highest standards of courage, and royals with the understanding that one great battle could bring them incredible riches. Henry would make it impossible for them to refuse battle today. His men-at-arms strode to within a couple hundred yards of the enemy and waited. His archers rammed stakes into the wet ground to help their defensive position on the right and left flanks while his nobles in the center unfurled the banners of the most distinctive families of Britain. As the English arrows began to fly, the French cavalry spurred their mounts forward, and their men-at-arms began their march into the English. King Henry V realized that the cream of French nobility was in the front lines of infantry, and that was as he wanted. He dismounted, drew his sword, and walked to the front. Live or die, today he would face the foe with his band of brothers.

It was October 1415, and King Henry V of England had come to France to assert his right to the French throne. Charles VI was reigning as the French emperor, but his bouts with madness had left him as little more than a figurehead. Having sailed across the English Channel, Henry V had laid siege to coastal Harfleur and done his best to bring the French to battle. The siege had accomplished very little, and his hope that King Charles would advance to fight had not come to fruition. The French were not fools, and only a fool allows the enemy to choose the place and time of battle.

With winter approaching and the campaign season ending,

Henry realized that his best option of survival was to march north to English-held Calais. His battlefield losses at Harfleur had combined with those from disease, and his army was only a reflection of what it had been as he set sail from England. The French understood his situation and checked his advances north, forcing his beleaguered army to wander south along the Somme River looking for an opportunity to ford. The French mirrored them from across the river, but would not bring themselves to battle. Why should they? Time was the friend of the French, and starvation and dysentery were as effective killers as French arrows.

The English were finally able to secure a crossing over the Somme, but their path was effectively blocked by French forces that outnumbered them at least four to one, with more arriving daily. Henry understood that his chances at a battlefield victory were slim, but he was also forced to accept the fact that he could advance no further. He stopped and assessed his predicament, considering the facts of the situation as it stood before him. His army consisted of about 5,000 English and Welsh longbowmen who would provide protection for his 1,500 knights and men-at-arms. It had rained for days, a primary consideration for his knights and nobles who would fight wearing full plate armor. To his benefit, his archers were more lightly clothed, most with helmets and with their bodies armored only by leather or padded cloth. These were also professional soldiers, capable of fighting in a measure of ways. Henry likely reflected upon the Battle of Crecy, almost 70 years prior, when the English had defeated the French with outstanding support from their bowmen. Given a choice, Henry would like to attempt that scenario once again, but the numbers against him made such a consideration almost impossible. He would almost certainly be flanked by such superior numbers, and his archers would be annihilated. They were fighting for their very lives, and Henry would have to find a perfect circumstance for even a chance at escape, much less victory.

On the French side were more than 20,000 royals, knights, men-at-arms, and archers. They were the cream of French royalty and led by Charles D'Albret, the Constable of France. King Charles VI had been fighting bouts of madness, so he and his eldest son had remained in Rouen as the French army had gone in pursuit of the English. While the French at Agincourt did develop a plan, the effect of the king's absence was that the royals had the ability to shift the conduct of the battle. In another period of history that fact might hold little significance, but in the 15th century there was potential for serious gain from the results of being victorious in battle. The practical reality was that a noble could be captured and ransomed for a veritable fortune, while the king, himself, would be worth more than might even be imagined. Hence the term "a king's ransom." Unlike the English who needed to force a resolution, the French could likely win simply by postponing the battle. But would their greed and arrogance allow them to do that?

Sometimes the most intelligent maneuver is to remain where you are and as you are. The French had done the shrewd thing by simply refusing to engage as the English gained their foothold across the river. They had the advantages of numbers, mobility, and the capacity to establish where the battle would be fought. Conventional wisdom of the day was to establish a line and to draw the enemy in to fight. The victor would inevitably be the troops who stood to receive the attack, and the French had the ability to dictate that.

The Battle of Agincourt is militarily notable for many reasons, but from a battlefield perspective we see significant mistakes by the French as well as ingenious tactics by the English. Of all the missteps the French made, though, their worst was their first: their selection of the battlefield. Having decided to give the English the fight they required, the French set their army between two heavily wooded areas. They did so, disregarding the fact that it would restrict their own mobility, while their enemy could use the forests to protect their flanks. Chalk up that decision as one of arrogance. The night before the battle the French lit campfires, told stories, laughed and joked, and contemplated how they'd spend their ransom. They knew how this battle would go and how it would end. In contrast, Henry, in fear of being surprised, ordered complete silence in the English camp. Any of the men-at-arms violating the order would have his horse seized, while the archers were told that disobedience would mean the severing of their right ear.

Arising on Saint Crispin's Day, King Henry found himself still in close range of the French and optimistic that he could force them into a fight. He gave his men a rousing speech, letting them know that for the rest of their lives they would be remembered in England, regardless of the outcome. Yet, as they stood waiting for hours on the French to accommodate them on the battleground, they realized that this was a stalemate. That would not do. Henry had divided his men-at-arms into three divisions and placed them in the center of his army, with his archers on the wings. He held a genuine hope that his men might remain static while receiving the charge of the French. But that was not to be. Henry realized that the French needed bait and some sort of provocation, so he ordered his entire force, archers included, forward.

While knights might be captured and ransomed, the archers understood that they were practically worthless as prisoners. Always susceptible to being overrun by heavy horse, the archers all knew that they would be killed if closely engaged. If there was ever an incentive to fire often and with accuracy, those English and Welsh archers had it. Set on the right and left wings of Henry's army, they steeled themselves for the French advance. Their advanced position still gave them the ability to anchor themselves on the woods, making it difficult for cavalry to flank them. They drove long protective stakes into the ground, designed to hinder knights on horseback, and waited.

Their wait wasn't long. The French cavalry deployed to the right and left and they advanced, numbering well over a thousand. Trotting at first, then galloping through the newly plowed field, they came smashing into the archers' pikes. Unable to break through, and with the woods impeding their charge, the French cavalry began to retreat toward its own lines. As they did, though, the 5,000 English archers gave them a parting shot. Tens of thousands of arrows were fired in less than a minute, and the exposed flanks of the horses began to burn and bleed as arrows struck their marks. The shrieks of the horses carried across the battlefield as did screams of outrage as thousands of arrows extended further into the lines of the French men-at-arms. So, just as the French lines were about to step forward, their own cavalry had come through in a disruption that might as well have been the enemy. Let me stress the point: The French cavalry had lost control and were galloping into their own foot soldiers. Men were knocked to the ground and the entire French force was drastically altered by this sudden interference of their own heavy horse.

Though their own cavalry had torn apart the structured assembly that would advance on the English, the odds were still overwhelmingly favorable to the French. In fact, the nobility practically jostled to be in the front of the first wave sent in. The British could see that the banners in the front rank represented the finest that France had to offer. The knights walking toward the English drew their swords, then closed their visors and looked to the ground so that English arrows would not penetrate their helmets.

Because the battlefield had been plowed, the recent rains had created a morass that was almost impassable. Beyond that, the French cavalry charge upon the archers had further churned the ground into a quagmire. It's beyond belief that the French nobles would continue with the charge, but on they came. The thought of riches played on their minds as the highest-born advanced in the first wave across that field. Even though the French had developed a plan for the battle, the reality is that this advance upon the English was not well orchestrated, and that these fully armored men were just walking forward shoulder to shoulder with almost no communication. The woods to their right and left kept them in a tight, almost immovable, formation, and the advance was up a slight incline, made more significant by the muddy conditions. Many soon found themselves knee deep in mud and struggling to continue the march forward.

As they got closer, focusing primarily on the royal banners and men-at-arms in the center, those who could advance were soon reminded of the power of the English longbow. The English Bodkin arrows could penetrate plate armor, and their strikes began to yield results among those coming forward. And yet they came. Henry V noticed that the cream of French royalty and knighthood were coming directly to him, so he dismounted and strode to the front. He had previously sworn not to be taken alive, and he relished the privilege of fighting in hand-to-hand combat. The sound of the battle axes and swords of men-at-arms proved that the French would not stop and that this battle would be hard fought. At the age of 16, Henry had been severely injured by an arrow while fighting rebels at Shrewsbury, and now, approaching 30, he would not shirk. His status mattered not. If need be, he would die alongside his men.

Having arrived at the English lines, French royalty wanted nothing more than the opportunity to capture or kill their English counterparts, with the king as the ultimate prize. And here we see what must be one of the most incredible scenes ever played out on a medieval battlefield. As the French second division came forward, a considerable number exhausted themselves before ever reaching the English. Many fell forward into the mud and drowned in their own helmets as their comrades marched atop them. But leading the second division was the Duke of Alençon, and he burst into the English line in a frenzy. He severely wounded King Henry's younger brother, the Duke of Gloucester, which quickly caught Henry's attention. Henry stood over his brother in a defensive position while the Duke of York also came to his defense. The Duke of Alençon was able to mortally wound the Duke of York, then swung his sword at Henry, knocking a fleuret from the king's helmet. Henry's Welsh bodyguard finally overpowered the Duke of Alençon, and as he was attempting to surrender himself to the king he was struck and killed. Many others likely met a similar fate.

But while the Duke of Alençon and dozens more were unable to surrender, other French royals were yielding by the hundreds and taken behind the English lines. As they were dragged to the rear, more came forward. The second wave began to falter, and men were finding it even more difficult to find space to use their weapons. More and more were falling into the mud and being trampled and drowned. The English archers recognized this as an opportunity. They flung aside their bows and rapidly descended upon the French. Many carried the hammers which they had used to drive their protective stakes, while others wielded knives or weapons picked up on the battlefield. Their lighter clothing made it possible for them to step through the mud, and they struck the French men-at-arms with a vengeance, killing thousands.

While the English seemed to be carrying the day—perhaps an hour had passed—the numbers were still against them. This was no time to relax. To their front remained thousands of French assembling to advance as a third division, fresh and ready to fight. To their rear were hundreds of captured knights and royals, worth a fortune in ransom, but in numbers large enough that they still might constitute a danger should they decide to dishonor their surrenders. Suddenly there came a hysteria through the ranks, as happens so often in military history when one side is so seriously outnumbered. The cause may have been a raid on their baggage train, which was in the rear, or perhaps a rumor that they had somehow been flanked by the French cavalry. Just the observation that the third division was stepping forward was likely enough to awake their fears and start a cry of panic, and King Henry felt the trepidation himself. In an act that exhibited the level of his fear, he ordered that all the prisoners be killed except for just a few of the highest ranking. This act seemingly violated the rules of chivalry, and his knights and men-at-arms refused to carry out the order. Finally, a squire and archers completed the grisly deed. I should make the point that Henry saw this act as a military necessity and one that cost him thousands of crowns in ransom. His killing of the prisoners was not criticized at the time, not even by the French.

The act worked to the benefit of the English in two ways. First, it eliminated any threat of the prisoners renewing the fight. Second, the sight was enough to dissuade the third wave from engaging at all. The French withdrew, the battle was over, and Henry was able to spare several hundred valuable prisoners. They were carried with him as he finally could make his way north to Calais and then back to England.

The Battle of Agincourt ended with English losses at just a few hundred, while French losses were possibly as high as 10,000. Constable Charles D'Albret was killed, as were so many of the royalty who had excitedly placed themselves in the front row of the advance. If battles were ever to be rated as upsets, this one qualifies as a top ten. In the days prior to the battle, the French had practiced self-restraint, simply blocking the escape route of the English. Then they became arrogant and compounded that arrogance with a poor choice of a battlefield. I have to acknowledge the fact that Charles D'Albret did put together a plan which included a flanking maneuver that could have brought cavalry to bear on the English rear. Encircling the English might have opened several possibilities, including an opportunity for the French crossbowmen to soften the enemy ranks before the men walked forward. Several knights even cautioned against carrying forward the battle as it unfolded, but they were disregarded by nobles with greed in their eyes.

Time had been their friend, but the nobles were filled with excitement and were just looking for an excuse to fight. The

English arrows into their ranks further angered them and provided an excuse to move forward when they should have just stayed with their plan. Simply put, their march forward was insanity. The return of the French heavy horse had disrupted their lines and they needed time to reform. The French also had thousands of archers, but they were given the opportunity to fire just once and then were never used again. The field was simply too narrow to accommodate the French cavalry, men-at-arms, and archers. That's another argument for a strategy that should have involved drawing the English into the open, or just blocking or surrounding them until they were forced to submit.

The absence of the French king at the Battle of Agincourt made this historic collapse more likely, as the seasoned commanders were unable to exercise control over those who wanted glory and gold. On the field at Agincourt, they marched onward through knee-deep mud and a slew of arrows to reach the English men-at-arms and archers. They died as barbed Bodkin arrows pierced their armor, as hammers smashed their helmets, and as knives were unceremoniously inserted into their visors. With them died the failings that had brought them to that point: greed, anger, excitement, and pride.

The final lessons of the French at Agincourt are simple. Control your temper. Don't be greedy. Understand when you're being provoked. Practice self-discipline. Choose your battles.

11

HAVE SOME FUN: THE BATTLE OF DALTON

"If we couldn't laugh we would all go insane."
Robert Frost

So, what's the point of all this? Many years from now when you're in that proverbial rocking chair, looking back, how will you rate your life? Was it a success? I hope you'll be able to say, "Absolutely, yes!" Did it turn out the way you planned? Probably not, because life doesn't work that way. Still, most of the responsibility falls on our own shoulders, for good or bad. The good news is that we always have the means to make improvements, usually immediately.

All my life I've known people who have set their ultimate goal of success far in the future. When they retire they're going to buy an RV and travel across the country. When the kids are grown they'll book that trip to London. They want a house on the beach. They'll write the great American novel when they can find the time. They'll reconnect with their spouse. You get the point and you certainly know where I'm headed.

Life's short. It's too easy to let it pass you by while you make plans. I preach hard work, discipline, planning, and focus, but I push those concepts so that you can get to what's truly important—the goals you've set for yourself and the things you'll want to see when you look back on your life. It's absolutely fine to have fun along the way. In fact, enjoyment of life, every step of the way, should be one of your priorities.

Take that European cruise, raft the Grand Canyon, enroll in a painting class, sign up with your buddies in the softball league, or go on that mission trip you always wanted to join. The balance between responsibility and fun can be difficult sometimes, but you can do it. I also want to stress that we each define fun in our own way, and you should do what you like. You should do it now.

*****

The Battle of Dalton — 1864

"Do not take life too seriously. You will never get out of it alive."
Elbert Hubbard

There's a saying that wars are started by old men and fought by young ones. That's true throughout history, and I would never argue otherwise. What I will do, though, is emphasize that young men will do everything in their power to keep some sort of normalcy. The ability to stay young and have fun matters, and I see that as an especially important thing—maybe even a coping mechanism—in warfare. Which brings me to my favorite battle of all time, one with few casualties but a tremendous amount of fun and camaraderie.

***

The winter of 1863-64 had been particularly bitter for the Confederate soldiers in the western theater. The bitterness, though, wasn't purely due to the cold weather. Confederate General Braxton Bragg had resigned his command of the Army of Tennessee in the winter of 1863, following strategic mistakes during the battles at Lookout Mountain and Missionary Ridge. Pushed out of Chattanooga, the Southern troops had fallen back to winter quarters in Dalton, Georgia. President Jefferson Davis appointed General Joseph E. Johnston to replace Bragg, and the men wintering in Georgia began to feel a bit more optimistic.

The cold weather had continued longer than normal, with the men still in winter quarters in March 1864. On March 22nd, the boys in gray woke to about five inches of snow, an oddity on a spring day in Georgia. Boys will be boys, and, after a quick breakfast, the fun started. The fun being, of course, snowball fights. There are several accounts of this "Battle of Dalton" in soldiers' diaries, so we know that small fights among camps quickly turned into men assembling themselves into larger, cohesive units. Some would go on the offensive, cheering and shouting, while others gladly played the part of the defending army. For the moment they could forget the Yankees to their north, making this battle Rebel versus Rebel.

Within an hour of rising from their shelters, 20,000 men were taking place in fights along a mile-long line. Accounts depict men stacking snowballs into pyramids six feet tall and waiting for their unsuspecting "enemy." Haversacks were emptied of rations and filled with snowballs. Handkerchiefs were tied to sticks to act as battle flags, and, in some cases, the actual Confederate regimental flags were brought out for the advance. Hillsides were held, valleys were contested, camps were raided, ground was hard fought and dearly gained. Prisoners were taken with severe penalties. A captured man might be taken to the ground with snow shoved into his shirt, into his ears, anywhere the captors laughingly wanted. Cavalry charged artillery batteries and infantry units teamed up against cavalry. The fun was contagious, and the citizens of Dalton came out to watch.

Confederate officers not only condoned this behavior, they participated. The men described their joy at seeing a certain colonel or major saddled up and leading his men into battle, colors flying beside him. Morale had been improving since the arrival of General Johnston, and the participation of the officers meant everything to the average man in the ranks. If there were ever a team building exercise in the Army of Tennessee, this was it.

I love to read wartime diaries, and this snowball fight is mentioned in several. A South Carolina captain described running for almost a mile trying to escape a Georgia soldier with madness in his eyes. A Texas lieutenant wrote of fighting against men from Mississippi and getting hit in the face with a ball that was more ice than snow. He believed that he had been half-blinded, and historical accounts imply that some men truly were.

Apparently, some of these snowballs were also constructed with rocks packed inside. Stupid, but certainly not out of the question for 18-year-old men.

The diaries also describe the larger movements, and those are intriguing as well. General Bate's Tennesseans, led by Colonel G.W. Gordon, attacked General Walker's Georgians; the 54th Virginia Infantry fought their brothers from the 63rd Virginia; General Patrick Cleburne famously led a brigade against his compatriot, Brigadier General Daniel Govan. Cleburne was captured, paroled, and recaptured. Threatened with a dunking in a cold creek for breaking his parole, he gladly bought his "freedom" with whiskey rations to those men from Arkansas. (Three cheers for General Cleburne quickly arose.)

The snowball fight at Dalton also is mentioned in several memoirs, written years after the war. Sam Watkins, in *Company Aytch*, gives just a quick mention of the battle. Relevant, though, was his memory of another event that happened that day. A deserter had been caught, tried, and sentenced to death by firing squad. Watkins, and others, included in their narratives that the man was given his punishment that morning. The snowball fight went on with barely an interruption. To the Confederate soldiers, death had become a normal part of life. The poor soul who left earth that day was merely an affirmation that life is fleeting.

I mention the execution as a reminder that we must accept the good and the bad, the happy and sad, as part of life. That's how it's served up, and that's what we have to deal with. The men playing that day knew that their days might be numbered, but they also recognized that a chance at a little fun was more important than worry. I'm glad they couldn't see the future: Atlanta, Franklin, Nashville. But that day, in that moment, they felt unrestrained joy.

Most people are about as happy as they make up their minds to be. Still, there are little things that help contribute to happiness. Do them. Take action!

Find some time to be by yourself, with family, with friends. Figure out how to do some of the things you've always wanted to do. If they cost money, then learn to save or find a way to pay for it. You can do it. If you have a bucket list, get started on it today.

Use your vacation days. Too many people never use their vacation days because they think it would "look bad," or because they "just have too much work to do." Do you think the company couldn't possibly keep going without you there for a couple weeks? Sure it can. The graveyards are full of indispensable men, as the adage goes. Vacation is earned, and it's absurd to leave it on the table while you have personal goals that could use that time.

If you hate your job, get a new one. One of the saddest things I've ever seen is when a friend despises his job, but is afraid to move on to something else. I understand the objections. Change can be frightening. You should also be frightened by the thought that you're going to waste the next several years doing something you hate. You have options.

Are you miserable in a relationship? Then fix it or quit it. I'm a firm believer that most relationships, if they were ever sound, can be fixed. I also believe that a strong commitment is a cement that can hold a couple together. Having said that, it takes two, and I've seen too many friends dealing with a partner who has no interest in the hard work it takes for a successful relationship. I have failed, myself. So, I know that you are not trapped. You have options. I'll say it again: If you want to be happy, the option is there. Fix it or quit it.

I want to do good in this world, and I want to spend my time, money, and efforts in accomplishing that. My grandmother always said that she would deem her life a success if she had made the world just a little better than it was when she was born into it. I like the way she thought, and I want to live by that rule, as well. Doing good and being happy are not mutually exclusive concepts.

I'm not releasing you from an obligation of doing good, or advocating selfishness or hedonism. I'm simply saying that you can, and should, be happy while you're making our world a better one. Do good, be good, be happy. Start there, and everything else will fall into place.

12

THE BATTLEFIELDS TODAY

Meuse-Argonne

Alvin York's amazing feats were accomplished near Chatel-Chéhéry in northeastern France, just to the west of Verdun. The area is rural, dotted with small villages, and is a great place to drive and explore World War I sites. The Alvin York site is in a heavily wooded area of the Argonne Forest, accessible by a two-mile loop path, which has signage so that you won't get lost.

There's a monument at the end of the trail and you can truly get a feeling as to how Corporal York and his men must have felt that day. There's a quaint WWI museum and a few hotels in nearby Verdun, and the historic little town also makes a great base for exploring the area. You'll enjoy Verdun and strolling along the Meuse River.

For further information on the location of the battle (and other cool stuff), visit www.sgtyorkdiscovery.com.

Culloden

The Culloden battlefield is in the far north of Scotland, just five miles east of Inverness. The battlefield is small and easy to understand, but offers a great walking opportunity. It seems as if the wind is always blowing through the heather and across the moor, and you can imagine the two opposing armies facing each other. The Highland Charge is easily pictured, with markers across the field designating everything from the front lines to burials. The museum is impressive and offers a modern (in a good way) interpretation of the battle, with interesting displays regarding clothing, weapons, and so forth.

Tours to the battlefield leave regularly from Inverness, so it's not a problem if you've taken the train. There are plenty of hotel options in town, as well as some great bed and breakfast homes along the River Ness (and elsewhere). You'll also find plenty of restaurants, pubs, bookstores, and such, but the place still has a small-town feel. I especially enjoyed the street signs in English and Gaelic.

Naturally, the big draw in the area is Loch Ness and the monster that has prowled it for centuries. There are also tours for that, and I highly suggest a boat cruise across the lake. One of the tours I most enjoyed was a boat ride down the lake, docking at the lovely ruins of Urquhart Castle, then by bus to the Loch Ness Centre and Exposition before heading back to Inverness. Also consider Fort Augustus and some of the smaller museums south of Loch Ness. You'll be glad you did.

The Culloden battlefield is maintained by the National Trust for Scotland and they have a great website at http://www.nts.org.uk/Visit/Culloden.

Cowpens

Cowpens is an incredible National Battlefield, just outside Gaffney, South Carolina. The National Park Service maintains its driving and walking trails and an interesting museum. It's possible to walk the field and imagine yourself running toward the British grasshopper cannons.

When you're in the area, don't forget that King's Mountain is just 45 minutes to the east. A National Military Park, it also has a great interpretive center and museum. The trail around King's Mountain is rugged, though, and is accessible only by foot. If you have mobility issues you'll find King's Mountain difficult, but I still suggest the visit just to get a feel for the terrain and to see the museum. Cowpens and King's Mountain combine for a great day of Revolutionary War history in the South Carolina backcountry. Cowpens information is online at www.nps.gov/cowp.

Hastings

If you're going to visit the Battle of Hastings site, you'll need to travel to Battle, England. Hastings is a great town on the coast, but the battle wasn't fought there. At Battle, though, you'll find a modern museum, a large gift shop, and the remains of the abbey built by William the Conqueror. Best of all you'll find a walking trail that takes you around the perimeter of the battlefield, with informative markers along the way.

While not exactly rural, walls have been built near the road so that the field maintains a sedate feel when you're inside the park. The museum includes some excellent interpretation and an interesting short film. It's a fun place for adults and children (very kid friendly), and I recommend at least two or three hours to properly visit. There's also a little cafe on site that I enjoyed. English Heritage maintains the battlefield and abbey, and they do an excellent job.

Battle is southeast of London, about an hour and a half by train. It has a dedicated stop, and the battlefield entrance is perhaps a mile walk from there. I also enjoy just walking around the old town. If possible, travel along the coast and visit Hastings, as well. Hastings has plenty of lodging options and may suit you better than smaller Battle. Pevensey, where the Norman invaders landed, is also a great little town to stop by for an hour or two (with a couple of amazing churches within walking distance). You can learn more by searching for Hastings on the English Heritage website at www.english-heritage.org.uk. I also recommend www.visit1066country.com for tourist information on Sussex and the coast.

Alesia

The Battle of Alesia was fought in what is now Alise-Sainte-Reine, in the Burgundy region of France. It's a rural area, northwest of Dijon. The hilltop is an interesting place and you can see forever from there. I can almost imagine Vercingetorix looking out to see whether his kinsmen were riding to help. Speaking of Vercingetorix, there's a magnificent hilltop statue of him there, erected by Napoleon III in the 1860s. (Some say that Napoleon III had the statue designed in his own image, and I believe that to be true.)

Nearby, there's a fairly new interpretive center that's very informative and highly recommended. They also seem to keep a good number of activities in the works. You can find them online at www.alesia.com. (There is an English language option on their site.) I recommend three or four hours at Alesia, as you need to visit the interpretive center, the hilltop, and the statue.

Alise-Sainte-Reine is one of those little out of the way places, with other small towns scattered around. I've always enjoyed simply discovering a quaint town and settling in for a night of small town life, and this is one of the best areas of France: wine country. If you're just touring the area and not sure where to stay, I highly recommend Beaune as a beautiful little town. The fact that it's in the center of wine country is a bonus, and there are often wine related events in the area.

Kortrijk

Kortrijk (Courtrai in French) is a large Flemish town in West Flanders, just north of Lille, France. The battlefield has largely been covered by urban growth, and there are just a couple references to the famous battle. Your first stop should be the Kortrijk 1302 Museum. It has some very interesting exhibits, multimedia displays, and helpful staff. You'll probably want to spend an hour in the museum, then let the staff give you directions to the Groeninge Gate and Groeninge Monument, which are located inside a small park that sets on part of the actual battlefield.

The walk there takes just a few minutes and is a casual trek through an interesting part of Kortrijk. The Groeninge Gate and the monuments inside were created for the 600th anniversary of the battle. Prominent is a large sculpture of a pair of spurs. Just a few yards away is an impressive gilded monument depicting the Virgin of Flanders. In one hand she holds a spear, pointed toward France, while in the other she holds the Flemish Lion, which has broken free of its shackles. The meaning is quite obvious.

For information on the museum, visit their website at www.kortrijk1302.be. For general city information go to www.toerismekortrijk.be. (Google will translate these pages for you.) I like Kortrijk, but it is a large city and it's easy to get a little lost. Store a map in your phone or pocket before you go.

If you prefer somewhere a little less metropolitan, Ieper (Ypres in French) is a marvelous little Belgian town, just 30 minutes away by car or train. Ieper is also a great base for WWI tours, with the awesome (kid friendly) Flanders Fields Museum in its reconstructed Cloth Hall. You absolutely should attend the Last Post service that takes place nightly at the Menin Gate. In fact, put that event on your bucket list.

The Alamo

The Alamo is in downtown San Antonio, Texas and is the most visited historic attraction in the state. The grounds are small, consisting primarily of the famous Alamo church, the Long Barracks Museum, and a large gift shop. Even though it is surrounded by all the hustle and bustle you'd expect in a large city, somehow the property maintains the propriety that it deserves. The church is cool, quiet on the inside, and one of the most solemn places I've ever visited. The Long Barracks Museum includes intriguing items such as one of Crockett's rifles, as well as an educational interpretation regarding the history of the property. I should note that there are also historic displays in the gift shop, so don't skip those. The grounds are walled and landscaped so as to continue the proper theme of respect.

Outside on the plaza is the spectacular Alamo Cenotaph which commemorates the men who fell there. We now know that the names listed on the memorial aren't entirely correct, but that takes away nothing from its magnificence. There are also other markers in the area to help give a feel where the walls were, and farther away you can find historical markers designating the placement of the Mexican cannons.

There is never a charge for entrance to the Alamo. Just show up during visiting hours. If there's a line, it generally moves quickly.

The Alamo grounds call for reverence, as do the staff. It's an educational place, but kids (and adults) need to be on their best behavior. Enjoy your visit for an hour or two, then finish with a stop at the gift shop. Buy a book, a Bowie knife, or coonskin cap to help keep the place operating. You can learn a lot in advance of your trip at www.thealamo.org.

Appomattox

Appomattox Court House is a small town of maybe a couple thousand people and an interesting place for a few hours. The battlefield has been preserved to a small extent, and you're able to walk hiking trails to the spots where the armies were when the surrender took place. The village was called Appomattox Court House, but the surrender was actually in the McLean House, just a few yards away. The property is maintained by the National Park Service and there's no cost involved. Start your tour at the courthouse building and then wander down to the McLean House. I should note that the McLean House is merely a reproduction of the original and does not have real historical significance other than where it's placed. You'll probably spend just a few hours at the park, even if you do decide to take one of the small battlefield hikes. There's also a small branch of the Museum of the Confederacy in Appomattox, which may be worth a couple hours of your time.

There are many Civil War related things to do in this part of Virginia and it's almost impossible to see them all. I recommend nearby Petersburg, as mentioned in the story, just a hundred miles to the east. The Petersburg National Battlefield has plenty for you to do and learn regarding the Siege of Petersburg. The Five

Forks Battlefield is about a dozen miles away, and, as a unit of the Petersburg National Battlefield, it contains most of the site where the April 1, 1865 battle took place. An interesting day would consist of Petersburg, Five Forks, then the drive west to Appomattox Courthouse.

Learn more about the current village of Appomattox Court House and what you'll see there from the National Park Service website at https://www.nps.gov/apco.

Bosworth Field

The Bosworth Battlefield is a half hour drive west of Leicester, England, near a small town called Sutton Cheney. It's a beautiful location with rolling hills and perfect vistas. The battlefield has a very good walking trail with informative signs regarding different aspects of the battle.

There always seems to be something going on at this location, from falconry to living history. It has a modern museum with a great staff. The cafe next door offers everything from coffee to a full lunch, all in an interesting atmosphere. Walk the trails, enjoy the museum, and plan on spending a few hours here. The hike around the battlefield is popular among locals, and you'll welcome their company. The museum has a marvelous website at www.bosworthbattlefield.org.uk.

A couple quick notes: Recent discoveries have me (and plenty of historians) convinced that the Battle of Bosworth primarily took place adjacent to the battlefield park. That location is visible from along the trail, though, and takes nothing away from the experience. Richard III is now properly buried in Leicester, and I recommend that town as a place to stay when visiting this battlefield.

Agincourt

Agincourt is in northern France, close to the Belgian border. The French (and correct, I suppose) spelling is Azincourt, so that's what you'll be looking for on the map. It's still a rural area, just a small town with a few hundred people. The battlefield is farmland and is almost pristine. The battlefield area is surrounded by local roads, so it's possible to drive or walk along the area where the French and English clashed. On one end is a small garden with interpretive signs and a monument to the French, but most of the actual battlefield is private.

Inside the village is a nice museum which features conventional storytelling signage, reproduction weapons and armor, battlefield representations, and modern media. The museum is absolutely worth a couple hours. They also have a little gift shop that I enjoyed. You can find details on their awesome website at www.azincourt1415.fr.

Agincourt, again, is small and rural, and seems to have just one restaurant. You may want to pack water and a snack if you plan on walking alongside the battlefield. It's a neat place and just a half hour drive from another Hundred Years War battlefield, Crecy. I recommend visiting both in the same day.

Dalton

The Dalton snowball fight happened in a fairly large area, but if you've ever driven on Interstate 75 to Atlanta from Chattanooga then you've been there. There's a spot on I-75 in Georgia where it crosses US Highway 41 in north Dalton. That's where some of the best fighting took place. It's also close to the creek where General Cleburne was threatened with dunking, as well as the spot where the deserter was shot.

I should note that the Confederates were holding Dalton for strategic reasons, and the Union army had probed their location during the winter. After the thaw, the Southern boys were forced to withdraw so as to keep themselves from getting flanked. Therefore, it's worth traveling down US Highway 41 (which basically parallels I-75) to visit Georgia Civil War sites such as Tunnel Hill, Dalton, Resaca, and Kennesaw Mountain.

Check out www.exploregeorgia.org for information on Georgia Civil War sites and other great places and events.

References

Meuse-Argonne

Sgt. York: His Life, Legend & Legacy: The Remarkable Story of Sgt. Alvin C. York, by John Perry. B&H Publishing Group, Nashville, TN 1997.

Alvin York: A New Biography of the Hero of the Argonne, by Douglas V. Mastriano. University Press of Kentucky, 2014.

The First World War – A Complete History, by Martin Gilbert. Henry Holt and Company, Inc., New York, NY, 1994.

The Tennessee Encyclopedia of History and Culture, by The Tennessee Historical Society. Rutledge Hill Press, Nashville, TN, 1998.

Bosworth

Bosworth 1485: The Battle that Transformed England, by Michael Jones. Pegasus Books, New York, NY, 2015.

The Wars of the Roses: Military Activity and English Society, 1452-97, by Anthony Goodman. Barnes & Noble, Inc., New York, NY, 1981.

The Wars of the Roses, by Terence Wise. Osprey Publishing, Oxford, England, 1983.

References

Hastings

1066: The Year of the Conquest, by David Howarth. Penguin Books, London, England, 1981.

The Battle of Hastings 1066, edited by Ken Osborne. English Heritage, England, 1994.

Hastings 1066: The Fall of Saxon England, by Christopher Gravett. Reed International Books Limited, Chatswood, NSW, Australia, 1992.

Cowpens

Cowpens: Official National Park Handbook, by Thomas J. Fleming. U.S. Government Printing Office, Washington, D.C., 1988.

A Battlefield Atlas of the American Revolution, by Craig Symonds. The Nautical & Aviation Publishing Company of America, Inc., Baltimore, MD, 1986.

It Happened in the Revolutionary War, by Michael R. Bradley. The Globe Pequot Press, Guilford, CT, 2003.

Duel in the Backwoods, by James K. Swisher. Military Heritage Magazine article, Herndon, VA, 2002.

Kortrijk

The Golden Spurs of Kortrijk: How the Knights of France Fell to the Foot Soldiers of Flanders in 1302, by Randall Fegley. McFarland & Company, Inc., Jefferson, NC, 2002.

Extreme War, by Terrence Poulos. Military Book Club, Garden City, NY, USA, 2004.

Alesia

Alesia 52 BC: The Final Struggle for Gaul, by Nic Fields. Osprey Publishing, Oxford, England, 2014.

REFERENCES

Caesar Against the Celts, by Ramon L. Jiminez. Sarpedon Publishing, New York, NY, 1996.

Julius Caesar, by Philip Freeman. Simon & Schuster, New York, NY, 2008.

Culloden

The Road to Culloden Moor: Bonnie Prince Charlie and the '45 Rebellion, by Diana Preston. Constable and Company Limited, London, 1995.

Culloden, by Phil Sked. National Trust of London, Edinburgh, 1990.

Like Hungry Wolves: Culloden Moor 16 April 1746, by Stuart Reid. Windrow & Greene Ltd., London, England, 1994.

Hastings to Culloden: Battles of Britain, by Peter Young and John Adair. Sutton Publishing Ltd., Stroud, Gloucestershire, England, 1996.

Agincourt

Agincourt 1415: Triumph Against the Odds, by Matthew Bennett. Reed International Books Limited, London, England, 1991.

The Hundred Years War: The English in France, 1337-1453, by Desmond Seward. Antheneum, New York, NY, 1978.

Appomattox Courthouse

April 1865: The Month that Saved America, by Jay Winik. Harper Collins Publishers, New York, NY, 2001.

Conceived in Liberty: Joshua Chamberlain, William Oates, and the American Civil War, by Mark Perry. Penguin Books, USA, 1999.

In the Hands of Providence: Joshua L. Chamberlain and the American Civil War, by Alice Rains Trulock. The University of North Carolina Press, Chapel Hill, NC, 2001.

References

To Appomattox: Nine April Days, by Burke Davis. Burford Books, Ithaca, NY, 1999.

The Alamo

Sword of San Jacinto: A Life of Sam Houston, by Marshall De Bruhl. Random House, USA, 1993.

Three Roads to the Alamo: The Lives and Fortunes of David Crockett, James Bowie, and William Barret Travis, by William C. Davis. Harper Perennial, New York, NY, 1999.

Lone Star Nation: The Epic Story of the Battle for Texas, by H.W. Brands. Anchor Books, USA, 2005.

Dalton

Confederate Diary of Robert D. Smith, by Captain James Madison Sparkman Chapter, UDC. Columbia, TN 1997.

Soldiering in the Army of Tennessee, by Larry J. Daniel. University of North Carolina Press, Chapel Hill, NC, 1991.

Diary of a Confederate Soldier: John S. Jackman of the Orphan Brigade, by William C. Davis. University of South Carolina Press, Columbia, SC, 1997.